WORSHIP

WORSHIP

by
John E. Burkhart

THE WESTMINSTER PRESS
Philadelphia

BOOK DESIGN BY DOROTHY ALDEN SMITH

First edition

Published by The Westminster Press®
Philadelphia, Pennsylvania

PRINTED IN THE UNITED STATES OF AMERICA
9 8 7 6 5 4 3 2 1

Library of Congress Cataloging in Publication Data

Burkhart, John E. (John Ernest), 1927–
Worship.

Bibliography: p.
Includes index.
1. Public worship. 2. Sunday. 3. Lord's
Supper 4. Baptism. I. Title.
BV15.B87   264   81–23116
ISBN 0–664–24409–2   AACR2

*To those with whom I have broken bread,
since they are companions for life*

CONTENTS

Continued

PREFACE

Christians gather for worship. Their assemblies may be small or large, and growing or shrinking from what they once were. The surroundings may be splendid or rude, the pace leisurely or busy, and the atmosphere boisterous or solemn. Worship takes many forms; and people may worship for a variety of reasons. They may come together out of some deep and durable devotion to the reality and worth of God, or out of some lingering sense of duty or guilt, or for mutual support in what they take to be an unfriendly world, or from the almost spent force of unquestioned and unreasoned habit and routine, or for unacknowledged and unspecifiable reasons unknown. Nevertheless, they do gather, and continue to gather, often without benefit of clergy or theologians.

The clergy, to be sure, sometimes worry about worship, and the theologians have not been totally silent. Many pastors have shelves filled with books about worship, books of services and rites, books on how to lead worship, how to improve worship, and even how—in the sacred lingo of the century—to make worship more relevant. The academics have been busy too. There are stacks of scholarly journals and more or less weighty volumes dedicated to precise understanding of how worship once happened. Much of this is interesting to avid liturgical hobbyists, and some of it, surely, is quite valuable in the shaping and reshaping of authentic liturgies. Note, for example, the impact of research into the *Apostolic Tradition* of Hippolytus upon the liturgical renewal imprinted in the more recent worship-books of the Anglican, Lutheran, Methodist, Presbyterian, and Roman Catholic churches. Nonetheless, for all their intrinsic worth, up-to-dateness, and general usefulness, such books do not appear to have solved all of the fundamental problems people have with worship.

In our time, as Paul Tillich so cogently recognized, the human questions are not basically those of practice but of meaning. Meaning is now the human question. No matter how busy humans become, or how practiced in their several occupations or diversions, an undertow of meaninglessness seems to unsteady all of their efforts. If such a reading of the situation is accurate, then the basic liturgical problem may be the unvoiced question of the real meaning of worship. What meaning does and can worship have now? Does it make sense, or is it ultimately a nonsensical enterprise? And if worship is a sensible activity, not simply touching the senses but intelligible and capable of making good sense, why and how does it make sense? And what sense does it make? Or have those who do worship simply taken leave of their senses? In a word, is there any discoverable theo-logic to worship?

The essays that follow are attempts to sketch a theology of worship. They are theological essays, efforts at some coherence about worship, written not so much to persuade people to worship as to help those who do worship to understand what they are doing. They are explorations in the logic of worship, arising in part from a conviction that much mischief is done by thoughtlessness. They are written simply to help those who do worship understand more clearly what they are about, and to this end are occasionally tendentious and provocative. Not all understanding arises from agreement. Nevertheless, insofar as worship may be described as a grateful recognition of reality, these thoughts are presented in an endeavor to expose a more than verbal kinship between thinking and thanking. Concern with the theology of worship draws upon material from many sources, and thinking responsibly about worship necessitates foraging in many fields. Hence, although these essays are theological in character, they incorporate evidence and insights from several anthropological, biblical, historical, and theological disciplines, as well as from a variety of liturgical experiences. Taken together, they explore ways in which Christian gatherings for worship may be understood as events wherein such ordinary human activities as assembling, observing times, eating and drinking together, conversing, and welcoming newcomers are occasions for the public celebration of God.

My personal acknowledgments to others are perforce brief, though those who are familiar with the resources upon which we all draw will recognize, perhaps better than I, the measure of my indebtedness and the limits of my understanding. The sheer weight of material with which a theologian of worship should be familiar is intimidating, even to the brash; and, like a seer surprised and overcome, I must confess that I have already glimpsed more than I can assimilate or tell. Indeed, were I to list all my grounds for gratitude, this modest book would become a bibliography, a map of communities of faith, and an autobiography.

Aside from thankful apologies to diverse scholars upon whose turf I have transgressed, my personal appreciations reach in many directions. I am grateful to those with whom I have lived and worked and worshiped for many years.

Beyond my immediate loved ones, special thanks go to my colleagues (students and faculty) at McCormick Theological Seminary. President Jack L. Stotts, Dean Lewis S. Mudge, Professors Edward F. Campbell, Jr., Robert C. Worley, and others have given more encouragement and wise counsel than I can repay. My thanks go to G. Fay Dickerson, who prepared the indexes. Various congregations of the faithful have helped shape my understanding of worship and have truly been means of grace to me. My thanks go to them, as well as to those students and teachers of social anthropology at the University College, London, who in 1972 coaxed me into the shared delight and recognition that humans must celebrate or die. My thanks go also to Rev. Thomas Smith, C.S.C., and that eucharistic community which is Moreau Seminary in Notre Dame, Indiana. They welcomed me into their home while most of these pages were being written, and I shall always be grateful to them for occasions noticed gladly. For them, and for others who are also remembered and cherished, thanks be to God.

JOHN E. BURKHART

McCormick Theological Seminary
Chicago, Illinois
After Pentecost 1981

Chapter
I

WHY WORSHIP?

"Serve Yahweh gladly"

Acclaim Yahweh, all the earth,
serve Yahweh gladly,
come into his presence with songs of joy!
                    —Psalm 100:1–2, JB

Accordingly all our life is a festival: being per-
suaded that God is everywhere present on all sides,
we praise him as we till the ground, we sing hymns
as we sail the sea, we feel his inspiration in all that
we do.
                    —Clement of Alexandria,
                      Miscellanies

          make bonfires
And feast and banquet in the open streets
To celebrate the joy that God hath given us.
                    —Shakespeare, *Henry VI*,
                      Part I

Only in rites
can we renounce our oddities
and be truly entired.
                    —W. H. Auden,
                      "Archaeology"

"Serve Yahweh gladly"

We live in a society where the value of almost everything seems to be estimated in terms of what it is good for. Nothing appears to deserve esteem simply for its own sake; nothing seems to have intrinsic value; and, for many of us, the world can be divided between the useful and the useless. In such a world, those who want to "get ahead" choose their friends, their goods, and their activities on the basis of what these can do for them. Under such circumstances, much of mutuality is simply a kind of shared selfishness; and in such a world, much of religious behavior can be understood as getting what one can out of God. It is scarce wonder, no wonder at all, that in a society dedicated to consumerism, people ask "What can I get out of worship?" As if getting something out of everything expresses an appropriate response to life! The question of worship, when so stated, does not take God seriously. It does not ponder the true worth of God, for to treat God as if God were a means to our ends is to imagine that we ourselves are gods. God is not humanity's servant.

I. What is worship? From time immemorial it has been suggested that humanity is God's servant. For example, in

the ancient Mesopotamian creation epic, Marduk resolves
to create "man," saying:

> He shall be charged with the service of the gods
> That they might be at ease![1]

According to this view, the gods really become gods only
when they are freed from the tasks and pressures of worldly
necessities. Servants make them gods. Gods are masters with
their lives enhanced by servants, and the more servants the
better. Even the Hebrew Scriptures continue with this mas-
ter-servant imagery, though God's needs are muted. Worship is an act of service to God, even though God does not
really need what humans offer. For the Hebrews, God is
God, whether served or not; and God deserves to be served,
not for any reward to God's servants but for God's own
worth. God does not require praise to be God; but as God,
God demands it by right of being God. Among the ancient
Greeks, Plato, in *Euthyphro,* suggested that the gods could
not, by their very nature, be affected by our worship. Since
they did not change, they could not be changed. They were
beyond change and flattery. What, after all, do you give to
someone who has everything? It was left to Thomas Aquinas, among medieval theologians, to take this argument so
seriously that he argued that worship is not for God's sake,
but for ours. To this, in the sixteenth century, Calvin responded that the proper adoration of God is the prime
purpose of Christianity *("Le premier poinct de la Chre-
stiente est dadorer Dieu droictement").* [2] And, in the twen-
tieth century, picking up the theme of adoration, Evelyn
Underhill speaks of a "disinterested delight" and a "total
adoring response."[3] By such lights, worship is truly a matter
of worth-ship. It is the adoring response to God as the center
of value, to God understood as intrinsic worth.

Nevertheless, even such refined notions may mislead, perhaps because they are so refined, as if God were an awesome and distant potentate, sitting in icy splendor and simply waiting to be praised. For Jews and Christians, however, worship is never truly directed to an indefinite God. For them, true worship celebrates the most definite God of the covenant in Moses and Jesus, the God of Abraham, Isaac, and Jacob, of Sarah, Rebekah, and Rachel, and of countless others. Fundamentally, *worship is the celebrative response to what God has done, is doing, and promises to do.* True worship thrives on the recognition that God and grace cannot really be thought apart. Since God *is* gracious, there is finally no genuine distinction between God's being and God's acting. They cannot be separated ultimately without doing violence to the character of God as given in God's gracious activities. Hence, all notions of worship which claim to honor God for God's self apart from God's gifts, as if such unprompted adoration were somehow superior to gratitude, reduce grace to a whim by making it uncharacteristic of God. For the peoples of the covenant, there is no God above, behind, or apart from the God who is gracious. Worship is response, and the God to be responded to in worship is the God whose grace deserves gratitude. God is not selfish; but, like any living giver, God-as-giver receives delight in our acknowledgment of the gifts God gives. Therefore, the appropriate imagery to understand worship is not the adoring obeisance of a servant for a master, but the grateful rejoicing of those who know themselves as genuinely befriended. The question that prompts worship is no longer, "What can you give to someone who *has* everything?" Rather, by God's grace, it has become, "What can you give to someone who *gives* everything?" With this question, the gifts are understood as offering occasions to honor the Giver! Thus, like The

Gospel According to Luke, worship begins in the recognition
and appreciation "of the things which have been accomplished among us" and quickly moves to honor the One who
has accomplished them. Or, as Langdon Gilkey puts it,
worship is "a response to the presence of the holy objectively
experienced in our midst."[4]

What matters, therefore, is not whether God can be God
without our worship. What is crucial is whether humans can
survive as humans without worshiping. To withhold acknowledgment, to avoid celebration, to stifle gratitude, may
prove as unnatural as holding one's breath. Martin Luther
took the story of the ten lepers (Luke 17:11–19) as an
example of "true worship." The one leper who was grateful
praised God. The event for which he was grateful became
an occasion to honor God. Indeed, some Calvinists were so
impressed with the story that they conjectured from it that
only one in ten was among the elect and would be saved.
Perhaps they were right, if only insofar as their theological
instincts led them to observe that finally the only line worth
drawing is that between the grateful and the ungrateful!

Since Christian worship is a response to the active, gracious, caring God revealed in Jesus as the Christ, there is no
longer any room for *cult.* There is no longer need to care
for the gods to free them from care. God does not need to
be tended to. Since the life, death, and resurrection of Jesus
and the destruction of the Temple in Jerusalem, there is no
time or place for the cultivation of God's favor. For Christians, through the firm testimony of God's Word and Spirit,
God's favor is sure. Therefore, since grace is a gift, Christian
worship is never other than a response. God has taken the
initiative, and worship understood as cult has ended in
Christ.

The impact of this upon the vocabulary of the earliest

Christians was astonishing. They lived in a world swarming with religions and permeated with cultic language. Surrounded by temples and shrines, priests and oracles, mysteries and sacred rituals, these Christians seem deliberately to have turned their backs to it all. For example, the important Greek term *hieros,* meaning "sacred" (as in hierarchy), scarcely appears in the New Testament. Other cultic words in the *hieros* family—words such as those for temple, priesthood, priestly service, reverent, or sacrilegious—are characteristically used to describe Jewish or pagan practices, are taken metaphorically to describe the life and work of Jesus or the daily lives of Christians in the world. Theirs was a daring linguistic move. Its import and impact may be appreciated if one determines that the Latin word *sacer* is henceforth forbidden, and if one tries to discuss religion without speaking of the sacred, sacraments, sacrifice, or sacrilege. Yet it appears, linguistically at least, that for the writers of the New Testament, cult and idolatry were virtually synonymous.

Nowhere is their renunciation of the cultic more obvious than in their references to *thysia* ("sacrifice"). For them, "what pagans sacrifice they offer to demons and not to God" (I Cor. 10:20). In Jesus, *the* sacrifice has been offered, the sacrifices of the Old Testament have been abolished, and

> we have been sanctified through the offering of the body of Jesus Christ once for all. . . . Through him then let us continually offer up a sacrifice of praise to God, that is, the fruit of lips that acknowledge his name. Do not neglect to do good and to share what you have, for such sacrifices are pleasing to God. (Heb. 10:10; 13:15–16)

The import is clear. God as God has provided the one and sufficient sacrifice. Sacrifice is God's gift to humans. Therefore, go with the grain. Christian sacrifice, the only sacrifice left, is sharing gifts with humans. Thank God and serve neighbors! Thus, although matters were soon to change—perhaps as early as the Didache, where the Christian gathering to break bread is alluded to as a "sacrifice" *(thysia)*—the New Testament itself nowhere makes such a connection and, indeed, seems even to resist it; and the table used is nowhere called an altar. It is simply the "Lord's table" (I Cor. 10:21), though the Greek fathers are soon to refer to it as the "sacred table" *(trapeza hiera)* and then later as the "altar" *(thysiastērion)*. Nevertheless, despite these later accretions, and in a world rife with sacrifice, probably the heart of the New Testament understanding of sacrifice is to be found in Paul's transformed use of the language of sacrifice in Romans 12, where he even plays with the terminology, so that sacrifice is not killing but living. As James Moffatt translated the passage: "Well then, my brothers, I appeal to you, by all the mercy of God, to dedicate your bodies as a living sacrifice, consecrated and acceptable to God; that is your cult, a spiritual rite." Because *the sacrifice* has already been made, our whole lives are to become a festival, to be celebrated in sincerity and truth (I Cor. 5:7–8). As a response to God's gifts, life is a continuous act of worship.

Therefore, among the traditional Greek words associated with worship, there are also changes in usage and meaning. *Latreia* had meant "ritual duty, service of the cult" (Heb. 9:6); among the earliest Christians, it came to mean dedication of everyday life to God, a reasonable "service" (Rom. 12:1). *Leitourgia,* which had meant public service, a work done for the people, and had come to mean cultic activities for the gods of civil religion, became among Christians charitable good works, such as the alms collected for the poor within the congregation at Jerusalem (Rom. 15:27) or the

missionary ministry of sharing the gospel with the Gentiles
(Rom. 15:16). Only in Acts 13:2 is the corresponding verb
(leitourgeō) used for Christian worship, where it seems to
refer to prayer. *Proskyneō* is the word most frequently translated as "worship" in the New Testament. It suggests a
posture of "bowing down before" which seems to imply a
directionality to worship. It was, therefore, suitable to describe pagan worship before sacred persons and shrines. Remarkably, therefore, while it appears frequently in the New
Testament, only once does it appear clearly to refer to worship within a Christian congregation (I Cor. 14:25); and
there, significantly enough, the divine presence is not in any
sacred place or thing or person but *among* a people.

Thus, the New Testament abandons or transforms the
cultic terminology, so that worship is no longer properly
understood as the ritual service of the gods. No longer is it
necessary to win their favor by attending to the sacred,
sacrificing, or otherwise serving them cultically. In the process, the New Testament also redefines the idea of service.
It chooses the commonplace, quite ordinary, "secular"
words *diakoneō, diakonia, diakonos* ("serve," "ministry,"
"servant"). The root imagery is of waiters at tables, minister-
ing to people's needs. The sense is clear. Since God does not
have the needs of the pagan gods, humans are released from
cultic functions and are free to serve one another. Such is
the import of the terminological shifts. Because of the service of Jesus in the world, the cultic logic for worship has
collapsed. Whatever function worship has, it is as a response
to God's work and is inextricably related to the Christian's
work in the world. As Ferdinand Hahn observes:

> The terminological evidence means not only that any cultic
> understanding of Christian worship is out of the question,

but also that there is no longer any distinction in principle
between assembly for worship and the service of Christians
in the world. . . . Worship in the sense of devotion to God
is by no means abolished; but this devotion does not take
place in a special defined area, but belongs in the midst of
the life lived by Christians.[5]

Second Corinthians 9:11–15 gives eloquent statement of
this profound relation between worship and service, as it
explores and illumines the intricate conjunctions between
grace, gratitude, and generosity.

Christian worship is a response to God's grace. As response, it is not cultic. Indeed, the very heart of the New
Testament's controversy with cultic thinking lies in the understanding of grace. Christian self-understanding is anchored in grace, while cultic activities parade as religious
achievements. In Paul's terms, the issue is simply grace
versus works. Christianity is not cultic. Christians do not
cultivate God. Rather, they know themselves as cultivated
by God. Worship, no less than believing, manifests the
delicate relation between grace and freedom, as those
"gifted" for worship give thanks for God's grace. Whatever
we give God has already been given us. Whatever we desig-
nate as holy has already been hallowed by God. Whatever
language, gestures, or patterns of worship we choose, they
have been granted to us in our time and place by a culture
formed with God's care. In everything, we have to do with
the living God. Such convictions are the matrix of worship;
without them, worship is meaningless. Therefore, as response, acts of worship are believing celebrations of what
God is about in the world.

II. Worship, understood as response, inevitably takes form in symbolic activities. Quite simply, *symbolic activities are actions that speak for themselves while pointing beyond themselves.* Like hugs and kisses, they do not need to be explained, certainly not by words, and yet they are carriers of meaning, often shaping our lives in ways of which we are not fully conscious. To be human is to act symbolically and to symbolize through actions. The most pragmatic humans alive engage willy-nilly in "useless" ceremonies, cultural habits, social customs, and rituals. Human life is marked, defined, and given shape by symbolic activities. Even such rudimentary social gestures as nodding a greeting, shaking hands, embracing, conversing, and waving good-by, represent social commitments of momentous significance and are styled according to cultural patterns of behavior. Friendships, various social relationships, business agreements, and religious beliefs are expressed in symbolic acts. As Suzanne Langer observed, human life "is an intricate fabric of reason and rite, of knowledge and religion, prose and poetry, fact and dream. . . . Ritual, like art, is essentially the active termination of a symbolic transformation of experience."[6] Within such a vision of life, rituals are not practical but expressive.

This way of understanding ritual was nicely articulated in John Beattie's 1965 Malinowski lecture on "Ritual and Social Change."[7] There he explored the question of the difference between "ritual" procedures and "practical" or "scientific" ones. His answer was that the characteristic and distinctive quality of ritual is "expressive." The primary question about ritual is not, "What does it do?" but rather,

"What does it say?" Ritual is essentially dramatic. It has a symbolic character, and functions in ways that practical activities do not. For Beattie, as for many others as well, the distinction between *expressive* and *instrumental* actions is crucial, even though much human behavior is at the same time both symbolic and practical. Fundamentally, ritual is to be allied with art rather than with science. Ritual, like art, is a way of saying things. Therefore, ritual is in its own way an end in itself. As dramatic expression, it is its own reward. The play is the thing, the play itself and not whose conscience it catches. Hence, for those who insist upon asking the utility question of rituals, their utility is located in their ability to express, to dramatize, through symbolic representations. For Beattie, rituals embody their own rationale. Their efficiency resides in their powers of expression. In Edmund Leach's lucid phrase, "we engage in rituals in order to transmit collective messages to ourselves."[8] Therefore, some social anthropologists say, if you would know a people, would know what motivates them, would know what they really care about, study their rituals.

Rituals, ceremonies, and even games, reveal the convictions a society has about life. For instance, wherever fathers still "give away" the bride at a wedding, the ties with patriarchy and notions of women as chattel have not yet been severed, no matter what may be said to the contrary. Or when, as Claude Lévi-Strauss reports, the Gahuku-Gama of New Guinea played football several days running until there were no losers and each side had the same score, they revealed the egalitarian and communal texture of their world view. Anthropologically (and theologically!), contrast this with "sports" in the United States, where football may be the major surviving public ritual, vigorously articulating the world view that aggressiveness, individual initiative, team effort, and winning are not only important but they are "everything"! Such symbolic activities, celebrated with enthusiasm, not only express but also legitimate and engender competitiveness as a way of life.

In any event, it is a commonplace now that students from modern technological societies tend to ask ethnocentric questions of another culture. Introductory anthropological textbooks often include references to the typical question: "You don't actually expect your ancestors to eat the food you've put out for them, do you?" But, obviously, the real question to be posed and probed is why modern societies seem uniformly adept at producing people who insist upon asking instrumental questions about expressive activities; and, incidentally, the answer might explain why artists and saints sense such alienation from industrial society. Instrumental questions seem natural to those whose ways of seeing and sorting reality have been shaped within a technological environment. This is patent. Furthermore, within a consumer society, there is almost inevitably a pervasive tendency to believe such clichés as "Everything has its price." For many in our time, it appears that nothing, literally nothing, is perceived as its own reward. We are pragmatically oriented, and "How can it be used?" is our usual question. No wonder that in such a world even religions become instrumental, as cults spring up to manipulate the gods!

Beattie's analysis of ritual is illuminating and theologically suggestive. However, when symbolic activities express relationships, something happens that transcends the simple opposition between expressive and instrumental. In relationships, to say something is to do something. In the deepest sense, one says love by making love. Relationships seek and find expression through symbolic acts; and symbolic acts express, sustain, and strengthen relationships. For example, a love between two persons may have been growing for months and years. At some point one of them hazards the proposal that they get married, celebrate with a wedding, and exchange rings. The giving and receiving of rings is an event in the lives of both of them, and in that new reality of their togetherness. The commitment is sealed by promise and gift, tell and show. The rings encircle the relationship. They represent a certain definiteness, a tangible band and bond of commitment, a commitment less retrievable than when it rested simply in the cloudy realm of protestations of love. The rings are a reminder to each and to the world of promises received and given. And, as symbols that something definitive has happened, they affect and determine something of the future.

Symbolic activities express; they also transform. They are performative. Ritual actions are empty neither of meaning nor of effect, and even their absence sometimes speaks. Note, for instance, that in the *Westminster Directory* of 1644, the Puritans stated, in discussing the Lord's Supper: "The Collection for the poore is so to be ordered, that no part of the publique worship be thereby hindred."[9] What a potent symbol! In one sentence, by this one act, they sundered sacred and secular, thereby separating worship and ethics. They gave a signal, fatal to biblical piety, that duties to neighbor were separable from and inferior to duties to God. Of course, the reason may well have been an experienced and reasonable fear that the traditional offertory bespoke a cultic piety, grandly meeting God's "needs" sacrificially; but among the consequences, doubtless unintended, was a divorce between the holy and the humane. In any case, they altered their symbolic behavior to match their thoughts.

However, the move is not always from thought to action, from theology to worship. As Clifford Geertz notes:

> Religious symbols formulate a basic congruence between a particular style of life and a specific (if, most often, implicit) metaphysic, and in so doing sustain each with the borrowed authority of the other.[10]

In rituals, humans express their faith, to be sure; in rituals, they also "attain their faith as they portray it." To participate in symbolic activities is always risky, for they open people to new and unthought possibilities. Religious rituals place "proximate acts in ultimate contexts." Contrary to common misunderstandings, symbols are not *merely* symbols. They are symbols, potently so. In Geertz' words, religious ritual

> alters, often radically, the whole landscape presented to common sense, alters it in such a way that the moods and motivations induced by religious practice seem themselves supremely practical, the only sensible ones to adopt given the way things "really" are.[11]

Symbolic activities, by completing and correcting the everyday view of reality, transform the ordinary into trysts with transcendence. Hence, worship is not only, in Panikkar's phrase, "those acts by which we express our stepping out of the banal";[12] it is also those symbolic activities in which we find ourselves, by God's grace, so reoriented that we realize (recognize and enact) what life really is. Symbolic activities not only express and perform, they realize life as hallowed by God.

III.   Worship is a graced response through symbolic
activities that *celebrate* God. The heart of worship, at least
for Jews and Christians, is the celebration of God. Its charter is Psalm 100:

> Acclaim Yahweh, all the earth,
> serve Yahweh gladly,
> come into his presence with songs of joy!
>
> Know that he, Yahweh, is God,
> he made us and we belong to him,
> we are his people, the flock that he pastures.
>
> Walk through his porticos giving thanks,
> enter his courts praising him,
> give thanks to him, bless his name!
>
> Yes, Yahweh is good,
> his love is everlasting,
> his faithfulness endures from age to age.
>   (Psalm 100, JB)

Every word is considerable, and together the words articu-
late a resounding definition of worship as celebration: acclaim, serve, gladly, presence, songs of joy, know, people,
giving thanks, praising, bless, Yes! This psalm is a veritable
lexicon of praise, whether in the Hebrew of the Masoretic
text, the Greek of the Septuagint, or the Latin of the Vulgate. It continues its force in the Siddur (Jewish daily prayer
book), where it is among the psalms recited daily; and it has
become memorable for many Christians in its metrical version sung to the tune "Old Hundredth":

> All people that on earth do dwell,
> > Sing to the Lord with cheerful voice;
> Him serve with mirth, his praise forth tell,
> > Come ye before him and rejoice.

Incidentally, in a curious divergence of this text, the English "serve with fear," while the Scots "serve with mirth"! Mirth is right, since worship is a glad response to the wonders of God's goodness, love, and faithfulness. In the felicitous translation of the Jerusalem Bible, worship is the celebrative "Yes" to God!

Among Jews and Christians, true celebration of God is quite festive, sometimes almost playful, and conspicuous in its gladness as it takes delight in what God is about. Ultimately, therefore, true worship is not solemn, since its proper gravity, its very seriousness, its correct decorum, is a graced gladness. Its sounds are a holy glee; and its silences are a still rejoicing "with unutterable and exalted joy" (I Peter 1:8). As the Calvinists put it at Westminster: "Man's chief end is to glorify God, and to enjoy him forever." Such worship celebrates God, the God known by prophets, psalmists, and apostles, and by multitudes of Jews and Christians, for whom worship is not a duty but a privilege, not a burden but a delight. Worship gladly celebrates the God whose character is caring and sharing, the God who is indecorously gracious. Therefore, *as celebrative response to such a God, worship has three dimensions. It acknowledges, rehearses, and proclaims.*

Responsible worship *acknowledges* God. It originates in the graced sensing that there is a worthy reality beyond ourselves; it grows in the gifted appreciation of who God is; and, at its summit, it is suffused with an overflowing enjoyment of God's graciousness, so that, on occasion, the notes of praise fairly tumble over one another, as in Rev. 7:12, saying "Amen! Blessing and glory and wisdom and thanksgiving and honor and power and might be to our God for ever and ever! Amen."

Amen! Worship which is responsive, responsive to God, and therefore responsible worship, commences and culminates in Amen, as Yes to God. Worship as acknowledgment is not simply knowing that God is real. Such knowing is not worship or even theology. Worship is responding affirmatively—accepting God, opening life to God, and rejoicing in God's transforming reality. *Blessing!* The Hebrew *berakah* and the Greek *eulogia* are words potent with meaning and power. Those who bless God ally themselves with God's causes; they venture and risk their own reality, siding with the worthiness of God's endeavors as their only sure worth. They not only wish God well, and speak well of God; but they affiliate themselves with God, making God's good their own and only good. Truly to bless God is to open ourselves to being reshaped by God's designs. *Glory!* Proper respect for God knows no bounds, since ultimately God alone is worthy to be blessed. Genuine worship recognizes God's glory *(doxa),* the weighty splendor and sheer worth of God. Yet responsible worship knows and acknowledges that God's glory is not an icy grandeur, distant and unapproachable. It is God's very glory that God is to be recognized as self-giving. God's glory is God's gracious presence, hallowing our lives. To acknowledge this hallowing is to worship God. *Thanksgiving!* Grace evokes gratitude. In thanksgiving *(eucharistia),* those who worship are grateful for all God has done, is doing, and promises to do. Yet it is not only giving thanks that matters, but being grateful. True gratitude is a way of life. And it is not simply thanksgiving for the gifts of life, as if they were all that mattered. Such gratitude would soon wither in adversity. At the center of a knowing *eucharistia* is *charis,* and the heart of "grace" is not gifts but the Giver. As acknowledgment, saying yes to God, affiliating with God, respecting God, and being grateful to God, authentic worship may share even the despair and hope of Habakkuk:

> Though the fig tree do not blossom,
>   nor fruit be on the vines,
> the produce of the olive fail
>   and the fields yield no food,
> the flock be cut off from the fold
>   and there be no herd in the stalls,
> yet I will rejoice in the LORD,
>   I will joy in the God of my salvation.
> (Hab. 3:17–18)

Responsible worship *rehearses* graced reality. Truly to acknowledge God is to recognize that God has designs upon the world. To worship God is to affiliate with God's cause. It is to go with, and not against, the grain of grace. It is to consent to the direction and pattern of God's design. As Gerhard Delling puts it:

> Christian Worship grows out of an altogether dynamic event; it refers to a salvation-*history* and is part of it—*everything that is done in worship, every event in the service, stands right in the movement of this salvation-history and participates in it* (and the reverse).[13]

Since God's will gives movement and pattern to reality, shaping history to its redemptive goal, worship takes on the dimension of rehearsal. It serves God by shaping and reshaping human lives to express what life is all about. God is to be served in life, everywhere and in everything. Therefore, as the practice of authentic life, worship moves beyond acknowledgment into rehearsal. It becomes a matter of discovering the plot, finding roles, developing and refining characters, and practicing parts, lines, and gestures, in the drama of a history graced by God. In this dimension, the dimension of rehearsal, therefore, worship is to be judged by whether and how it transforms those who worship. This, though for different reasons, was the point Thomas Aquinas made about worship. Worship changes humans. It honors God and helps humans; and, because God's character is to share, the two are somehow interrelated. Note, for example, the intricate relation between the glory of God, worship, and hospitality in I Peter 4:7–11! As Paul reminded the Corinthians, who seemed dedicated to severing worship from neighborliness, worship is to be conducted "so that the church may be edified" (I Cor. 14:5).

The participants in the rehearsal—given enough time and space for tryouts and rehearsals, groping and growing, learning their lines and forgetting them, being prompted and remembering again, defining a character, stepping out of character and stepping back in, doing and redoing scenes, upstaging one another, meshing with one another, coaching one another, standing back for a moment, or even sitting offstage for a while to view the whole scene, and then stepping into their roles again—may find themselves caught up in the action, forgetting themselves, the scattered selves they were, and, even if only for a few moments, may find themselves transformed. In time, by grace and effort, they may become so accustomed to their practiced roles that they really become what they had only imagined. Incidentally, perhaps this means that the question of hypocrisy is not whether people act, pretending to be something they are not yet, but whether they are being transformed in the process, becoming the roles they had played. In this sense, gatherings for worship are dress rehearsals of life lived by the grace of God, lived like

> music heard so deeply
> That it is not heard at all, but you are the music
> While the music lasts.[14]

Responsible worship acknowledges God, rehearses life as graced reality, and *proclaims* the world as hallowed. Truly to acknowledge is to declare. Unless acknowledgment is tongue-tied, it announces. Since truth, by its very being, is public, and since worship tells the truth, worship dares not stay sequestered. Worship is never a conspiracy of silence. Responsible worship is a public event. In the New Testament, for example, even the language of worship is not "sacred" but public; and, at Corinth, according to I Corinthians 14, outsiders might enter the assembly. Also, as Robert J. Ledogar notes at the conclusion of his linguistic study of early worship texts:

> The basic praise-verbs in the Christian vocabulary originally had in common the sense of a public act, a proclamation before witnesses of the qualities and deeds of God. As expressions of thanksgiving these words imply a making known or recalling to the assembly of the things that God has done for man.[15]

One dimension of worship is this need, this gift and task, to tell the world the truth about itself and what has already happened to it. All of life—troubled or trivialized, serene or splendid, as it sometimes is—has been created by God and is already being restored, drawn together, and made whole. Worship serves as a living monument to what God has done, is doing, and will yet do, with the world. As Karl Rahner reminds us, it is precisely because the "world is permeated by the grace of God" that worship erects "a landmark, a sign of the fact that this world belongs to God."[16] In responsible worship, graced humans enact living testimonies to the reality of God's work in the world.

God is at work, graciously and wisely, even among those who do not know or acknowledge God. Their ignorance and ingratitude are not ultimately decisive. God will have God's promised way with the world, and those who acknowledge God's will and pattern their lives after God's way are summoned to share witness. Their worship calls attention—through people, acts, and words—to what is really going on in the world. As their worship proclaims, it alerts the world to God's designs upon it. Worship points not so much to God's presence as to God's activity. To be sure, as Langdon Gilkey has affirmed so instructively, worship is "a response to the holy objectively experienced in our lives." Nonetheless, as he, the author of *Reaping the Whirlwind*, a treatise on history and providence, would surely agree, worship is a response and testimony to that "presence" which transforms the present in its being present.

In his remarkable book on festivity, Josef Pieper proposes this definition: "To celebrate a festival means: to live out, for some special occasions and in an uncommon manner, the universal assent to the world as a whole."[17] That is a tall order; and few, other than Margaret Fuller, can so heartily "accept the universe!" Surely the universe as we know it has not earned such indiscriminate affirmation. Yet for all that, we experience, affirm, and declare God only on occasion, at particular moments, activities, and events. Our celebrations are occasioned by particular realities so recognizably hallowed by God that only worship makes sense as we "serve Yahweh gladly."

Chapter
II

THE LORD'S ASSEMBLY

"God is really among you"

Praise the Lord!
Sing to the Lord a new song,
   his praise in the assembly of the faithful!
                    —Psalm 149:1

But if all prophesy, and an unbeliever or outsider
enters, he is convicted by all, he is called to account
by all, the secrets of his heart are disclosed; and so,
falling on his face, he will worship God and declare
that God is really among you.
                    —I Corinthians 14:24–25

There is no life that is not in community,
And no community not lived in praise of God.
                    —T. S. Eliot,
                       "Choruses from *The
                       Rock*"

And so hasten to the assembly where the Spirit
abounds.
                    —Hippolytus,
                       Apostolic Tradition

"God is really among you"

Since the destruction of Herod's Temple and the fall of Jerusalem in A.D. 70, Judaism and Christianity have learned to live in dispersion from Zion. They have wandered, moved, and been scattered throughout the peoples of the earth. Among many Jews, despite the persistent Passover hope of "next year in Jerusalem," return—"going up" to Jerusalem—has usually meant simply the *aliyah* of ascending to the synagogue desk to read the Scriptures. For millions in the Diaspora, the Torah has become a kind of portable Temple. Christianity, meanwhile, appears basically to have relativized the very notion of sacred places. There have, of course, been pious flirtations with holy cities, pilgrimages, sees, and shrines; but all such temples tend to totter, especially under the weight and pressure of Paul's undying question to the Corinthians: "Do you not know that you are God's temple and that God's Spirit dwells in you?"

The ancient world was filled with "houses of God," dwellings for deities who could be visited and worshiped there. Fashioned lavishly or humbly, often on mountains or in groves, and tended by priests and other functionaries who cultivated the sacred, such shrines were attractions to the devout, since they promised the presence of the divine. The sacral religions of antiquity were often preoccupied with sacred space, place, and direction. Many honored the sun and its rising in the east. Hence they "oriented" their temples and shrines, celebrating in stone the directionality of their devotions, since "orient," "east," and "rise" were linguistically one. Prayers rose and set with the sun, as piety faced the sacred. Such religion seems almost archetypal, and may explain why even the Gothic cathedrals were built like ships, with their naves pointed toward the east, and their altars at the east end. Yet with the Copernican revolution, the very notion of orientation became disoriented. Since the sun no longer "rose," people stopped caring which way was east and began to wonder which way was up! In the modern world, Christians and Jews, scattered peoples, with only themselves as temples, gather to house God's presence. For them, sacred places are inevitably secondary to a holy people.

I.   Among the Jews the primordial act of worship is the act of assembling. The synagogue, basically, is not a building but a gathering. It is a congregation of people. Not so much an institution as an event, it is the activity of coming together. Religion is not what one does with solitariness; it begins in the move to overcome solitariness. Judaism lives in a social sense of reality. Therefore many of its religious ceremonies require a *minyan,* a quorum of ten men. According to the Mishnah, "If ten men sit together and occupy themselves in the Law, the Divine Presence rests among them, for it is written, *God standeth in the congregation of God.*"[18] Rabbinic understanding of Psalm 82:1, drawing upon the uses of the word "congregation," "assembly," or "council" *(edah, synagōgē),* argued that it took ten adult males to constitute an "assembly of God." In any event, whatever the composition of the group, the point is clear. God's presence does not require special places or sacred personnel. There is no need for buildings or rabbis to hold religious meetings. A group gathers and the prayers are said, using the plural "we" on behalf of the whole people. Worship is made authentic by gathering and by the divine presence promised to devout assemblies. Indeed, God and social solidarity are so related that, even when one prays alone, the plural "we" is used in the prayers; and, according to the Talmud, anyone who prays in disregard of another's prayers has his prayer "torn up before his face."[19] The assembly of God, the synagogue, links care for God inextricably with care for neighbor. Judaism knows well the recovery of humanity through assembly.

This profound sense of assembly doubtless goes back to the formative events in Israel's history; and surely at the heart of those events is the covenant assembly at Sinai, where "a mixed company of strangers" (Num. 11:4, NEB) were constituted into a people. At Sinai, according to Exodus 19–24, the Israelites became a people, received the charter of their existence as a people, and promised their allegiance to God's sovereignty. The covenant was a theopolitical event, creating new relationships and obligations. The relationships are with God and among the people; and the obligations are social and economic, as well as cultic. Because God is acknowledged to be a jealous God, nothing, whether public or private, is outside the realm of the covenant. Issues of worship, work, society, property, leisure, and family are all interrelated; with no lines drawn between the sacred and the profane. It was a covenant—not a contract but a comprehensive commitment; not a private affair but a public event; and not only a "religious" matter but a *totality,* since life itself is integral. This covenant was epochal for Israel's self-understanding, and Israel continued to look back upon it as "the day of the assembly" (Deut. 9:10).

The basic word for "assembly" in the Hebrew Scriptures is *qahal*, which may be translated as assembly, congregation, convocation, crowd, horde, host, or multitude. It indicates a human gathering, people assembled for political, religious, social, or military purposes. In the Septuagint, *qahal* is usually translated as *ekklēsia*. The translation is apt, for *ekklēsia* was a common term in classical Greek, used by such writers as Herodotus, Plato, and Aristotle to refer to public assemblies, gatherings, meetings of citizens—often for political purposes. Such is the meaning of *ekklēsia* in Acts 19: 23–41, where the reference is clearly to a public assembly of citizens, gathered to resolve a problem of relations between business, politics, and religion!

It is this word *ekklēsia*, the common word for "assembly," which the New Testament uses more than one hundred times to refer to the gatherings of Christians. Other words for gatherings, especially those with a cultic flavor, seem to have been avoided, perhaps deliberately. Christians assembled, not as a mystery society but as citizens of the realm, God's realm, the only realm that really mattered. As such, their very gathering was, like the *qahal* of ancient Israel, a theopolitical activity. Indeed, they were persecuted precisely because such assembling was rightly perceived as a political event and as a threat to the established authorities. They *assembled* for worship, and in that assembling these Christians expressed the reality of their common commitment. Their very assembling was itself their primordial act of worship.

Thus, in a way which the word "church" scarcely captures, the Bible speaks of *assembly* (whether as *qahal* or as *ekklēsia*). Too often, unfortunately, our language has emptied the *ekklēsia* of its eventful character. Notice, for example, the difficulty of translating *synerchomenōn hymōn en ekklēsia* (I Cor. 11:18). The Revised Standard Version has "when you assemble as a church," as if a religious institution were being created by association. The New English Bible has "when you meet as a congregation," which is a bit more specific, and poses the nice question whether Paul ever meant other than the congregation when he speaks of *ekklēsia.* In other words, did Paul ever imagine the *ekklēsia* as anything above and beyond specific gatherings of Christians in various localities? The Jerusalem Bible has "when you all come together as a community," which surely introduces one of the most ambiguous words in any language. The New American Bible simply says "when you gather for a meeting," and that catches the sense: when you come together in an *assembly!* Words like church, congregation, and community are too problematic, too heavy with the connotations of the centuries. They say too much and too little. The people are the assembly when they meet together. Such surely was the force of the Septuagint, where Judg. 20:2 speaks of an event *en tē ekklēsia tou laou tou theou* (in the assembly of the people of God).

In our discussion of the New Testament understanding of the assembly, attention needs to be given to words that refer to the act of assembling. Two crucial words are *synagō* and *synerchomai.* Both have the significant prefix *syn-* ("with"). *Synagō,* from which the word "synagogue" comes, means to assemble, bring together, gather. It appears about sixty times in the New Testament, especially in the Gospels and Acts, and perhaps most notably in Matt. 18:20: "For where two or three are gathered in my name, there am I in the midst of them." *Synerchomai* means to come together, assemble, meet. It appears about thirty times in the New Testament, most frequently in Acts and I Corinthians. "What then, brethren? When you come together, each one has a hymn, a lesson, a revelation, a tongue, or an interpretation" (I Cor. 14:26). The same verb occurs in I Cor. 11:20, which is translated in Today's English Version: "When you meet together as a group, you do not come to eat the Lord's Supper." This verse is especially instructive, since the words "as a group" translate the curious phrase *epi to auto,* which occurs about ten times in the New Testament, usually in relation to the assembly of Christians (see Acts 1:15; 2:1, 44, 47; I Cor. 14:23), and seems to be a technical term to suggest the intensity of relatedness when Christians gather *together.* Thus, from the words used to describe their assemblies, it appears that the earliest Christians understood themselves as coming together, gathered and brought, into a shared selfhood, graced and lived together in the presence and praise of God. This surely was what their assemblies were all about. Indeed, for them their very being together was so *symbolic* of their vision of reality made one through Christ that even the thought of isolated virtue was *diabolic.*

II.   Unfortunately, assembling for worship appears to make little sense to many in our society. The statistics are patent. For countless humans, congregating to worship has no obvious or compelling rationale. In fact, under the combined impact of industrialism, urbanism, pluralism, and technology, the very frequency, patterns, and purposes of all human gatherings have been affected. If humans are political animals, many would now seem to lack any interior sense of that reality. Ironically, just at the moment when ecological truths and nuclear threats have made the recognition of human interdependence imperative, most expressions of that interdependence are treated as if they were simply superfluous amenities, nice enough to have about, perhaps, but scarcely critical to survival. In a word, most of us now live most of our lives within an ethos of practiced indifference to realities beyond the congenial horizons of our several selves.

Individualism is assumed and esteemed today in ways and in measures which would have seemed idolatrous to the ancient Hebrews, idiotic (literally!) to the ancient Greeks, and traitorous to the ancient Romans. In our vaunted discovery of the individual, freedom has been equated with independence, covenant has been marked down as social contract, and social organization has been reduced to more or less voluntary associations whose membership results simply from acts of joining. Under such circumstances, even the term "membership" is no longer an accurate category, since it connotes a kind of belonging in which the group is prior to the individual. The earlier logic of membership in the corporate sense was cogently expressed in the *Didascalia Apostolorum:* "Now when thou teachest, command and warn the people to be constant in assembling in the Church, and not to withdraw themselves, but always to assemble, lest any man diminish the Church by not assembling, and cause the body of Christ to be short of a member."[20] Obviously then, as now, pastors needed to exhort the faithful to be faithful in attendance. What is noteworthy is the assumption that absence from the assembly was a loss of greater moment to the body than to the member. Social tissues mattered, and mattered greatly. Assembly was simply the expected expression of corporate life, since being human was understood as basically relational.

More recently, without this covenantal matrix, individual worth has tended to assume almost cultic proportions, while much religion has come to signify, in William James's definition, *"the feelings, acts, and experiences of individual men in their solitude, so far as they apprehend themselves to stand in relation to whatever they may consider the divine."*[21] The modern stress is upon religious living as personal piety and devotion to God, independent of communal disciplines and separate from the ventures and vexations of life in society. Under the aegis of individualism, the trends from the public to the private, from the corporate to the personal, from the social to the solitary, are conspicuous today. Aside from the vestigial cults of civil religion, whether in the United States or in the Soviet Union, piety in modern society is usually consigned to the private sector. Thomas Luckmann's thesis in *The Invisible Religion* is quite pertinent. Secularism has not so much stifled religion as driven it into seclusion. It has been privatized. Many in our time have turned inward to the isolated solaces of meditation, transcendental or otherwise, making solitude the sanctuary for the divine in their lives. Wherever individualism is assumed to give a sufficient reading of human being, gatherings for worship are dispensable options and religion becomes a private affair.

Compartmentalization, as Durkheim noted, is a consequence of the division of labor in modern society. As religion and society have been sundered by individualism and specialization, piety has been marginalized, relegated to a compartment in life. For many, total life values have become part-time norms. As business, politics, and science have filed their claims to vast areas of the cosmos, the "sacred canopy" covers less and less human space. For many now, as in the Hellenistic age, everything but personal morality and the fate of the soul has been relinquished to the powers of this world. Religions have surrendered their global functions. Life, in such a world, is composed of sundry things, all sundered from one another.

Religion, under the impact of individualism and compartmentalization, has become privatized. Its pieties are familial at best, cozily congenial, and scarcely venturing beyond the friendly intimacies of the familiar. Even the lines between city and suburb may mirror a mentality that separates private from public life, leisure from work, family from business, religion from politics, poetry from prose, fantasy from fact. In contemporary society, for countless millions, churched and unchurched alike, religion has become an occasionally attractive hobby, lingering on the fringes of reality. It lives its quiet and verdant life amid golf, bridge, and family picnics; and its gods, like the deities of the Hellenistic world, are known only to those who make their private retreats, looking for a deity who dwells far from the messiness of everyday reality. In such a schizoid world, religion chooses the quiet margins of reality, preferring contemplation to action, *otium* ("leisure") to *negotium* ("business"), and enjoys meeting its gods in gardens alone.

Religious consumerism is the consequence, and assembling for worship loses any rationale other than pious selfishness. A reading of reality that individualizes humanity and compartmentalizes religion gives worship the task of cultivating the self. As John Locke put it:

> Let us now consider what a church is. A church, then, I take to be a voluntary society of men, joining themselves together of their own accord in order to the public worshipping of God, in such manner as they judge acceptable to Him, and effectual to the salvation of their souls.[22]

Such religion no longer expresses or constitutes true social bonds, but serves finally to affirm, enhance, and enshrine attachment to ourselves as private persons. Within such a view of reality, the socially inclined become joiners, associating themselves with others for mutual benefit. Hence, many people appear to choose religious associations in the same ways they select other leisure activities, in terms of interests and satisfactions. Consequently, the so-called "successful" congregations tend perforce to become rather loosely textured associations of assorted individuals and families, seeking similar diversions, duties, and delights. In order to survive, many congregations seem to have acquiesced in, or even catered to, the pervasive consumer orientation of modern industrial societies, while their adherents seek a "faith that satisfies," join "the church of their choice," and evaluate worship by whether they "get anything out of it." Consumerism has become the order of worship for the day. Spawned by individualism and nourished in compartmentalization, the cosmology of consumerism renders senseless any assemblies for worship whose logic is other than ganging up to get a proper purchase on God's favor. Such religion becomes a club, using the force of numbers to coerce God. Ultimately of course, such victories are of short duration, since consumerism finally founders on the truth that worship and selfishness are incompatible.

III.   In the biblical reading of reality, individualism is demonic. It is literally diabolic, breaking covenants, rupturing relations, and sundering humanity from itself. From the garden to the city, from the initial "It is not good that the man should be alone" (Gen. 2:18) to the new Jerusalem which unites the nations (Revelation 21), the Bible is the story of peoples. The basic metaphors are not private but public, not personal but political. According to Genesis, not an individual but humanity, male and female, images God. God creates, chooses, covenants with, suffers with, struggles with, and restores a people. The name "Israel" is itself relational. Israel strives with God.

In the New Testament (apart from conjunctions, prepositions, pronouns, and verbs; aside from the ordinary words for day, earth, hand, heart, heaven, man, name, woman, word, work, and world; and beyond such obvious theological terms as faith, glory, god, grace, holy, law, sin, and spirit) the words most frequently used are all relational. They are, in order of frequency, the words for lord, father, son, brother, disciple, and messenger. Their only rivals, interestingly enough, are the words for city, crowd, kingdom, nation, and people! The biblical idiom is sociopolitical. It perceives persons in the terms of their relationships; and its God is the Lord who creates and restores a people.

Hence, for the Bible, dispersion is a curse and gathering is a blessing. The Hebrew Scriptures see dispersion as God's judgment. It is the "horror" that results from disobedience to the covenant (Deut. 28:25). Those who violate the covenant provoke God to anger, and will be punished. According to the Septuagint, this horror is *diaspora.* Diaspora is punishment. "And the Lord will scatter you among the peoples, and you will be left few in number among the nations where the Lord will drive you" (Deut. 4:27). Diaspora, to be scattered, is slaughter; it is death by dismemberment (Jer. 25:34). Or, as the New Testament has it, those who were dispersed "came to nothing" (Acts 5:36). For the Bible, to be dispersed into solitude is to know the deathly terror of nothingness. To be alone, ultimately alone, is to be desolate, deprived of everything that makes life human.

Yet the God of Israel who scatters also gathers. The loneliness of exile is overcome in assembly. To be gathered is to be saved. In the words of the psalmist:

> Save us, O LORD our God,
>   and gather us from among the nations,
>   that we may give thanks to thy holy name
>   and glory in thy praise.
>
> (Ps. 106:47)

Hence to this day, in the daily "Eighteen Benedictions," every devout Jew blesses the Lord and prays: "You are praised, O Lord, who gathers in the outcasts of His people Israel." Every synagogue is living testimony to God's saving purposes and powers; and every *minyan* gives proof that God has not abandoned the covenant nor forsaken Israel. In the messianic age the exiles will return, and their return, according to Isaiah, will be a sign to the nations:

> He will raise an ensign for the nations,
>   and will assemble the outcasts of Israel,
>   and gather the dispersed of Judah
>   from the four corners of the earth.
>
> (Isa. 11:12)

This prophetic dream is echoed and universalized in the New Testament, where Jesus dies "not for the nation only, but to gather into one the children of God who are scattered abroad" (John 11:52). According to the vision of Ephesians, "God's plan, which he will complete when the time is right, is to bring all creation together, everything in heaven and on earth, with Christ as head" (Eph. 1:10, TEV). This vast recapitulation promises to gather, to sum up, the whole universe under his lordship. Assembly is here transmuted into membership, membership in the body of Christ. Such vast ecological imagery, immense in implication and cosmic in comprehensiveness, humbles and hallows any and every assembly that presages the reign of God. Hence, while the assembly is not the kingdom, it is a harbinger of the kingdom, and it can pray in the words of the Didache, "As this bread was once scattered over the hills and being gathered together became one, so may your assembly be gathered together from the ends of the earth into your kingdom."[23]

IV. Christians are assembled to *celebrate* what God has done, is doing, and promises to do in the world. In their act of gathering, they recognize themselves as gathered, gathered by grace. That they assemble, being gathered and gathering, is a celebration of the social reality of God. Their primordial act of worship is their graced activity of coming together. Before they do or say anything, they have done this. They are assembled. Although their gatherings may and do resemble many other human associations congregated for amusement, improvement, or service, and although their motives for gathering are often mixed, their distinctiveness, their authentic rationale for being together, resides in their shared sense of reality as somehow graced, defined and transformed, in Jesus of Nazareth. Their alliance with him is the decisive clue to their uniqueness. They gather as Christians because they know themselves as associated in him.

As Christians assemble they *acknowledge* God's purposes to unite all things. Their gatherings arise from their common discovery that humans are bound together. Their sense of reality, given in Jesus, brings them to recognize the divinely intended interdependence of all things. Because "in him all things hold together" (Col. 1:17), they celebrate the very coherence of the cosmos by assembling. In such a world, assembling makes sense. It is an intelligent activity, going with the grain of reality. It is the primal event which celebrates meaning as a social reality and social reality as meaningful. For Christians, as for Jews, coming together is an ontological event, it is a metaphysical activity, it is a statement about the very design of reality. Whatever else they do or say, or fail to do and say, together or apart, Christians as Christians commence by assembling to acknowledge reality as graced and becoming united in Jesus of Nazareth.

As Christians assemble they *rehearse* life lived within the unitive purposes of God. In coming together, being gathered and gathering, they not only acknowledge but also enact a vision of reality. They have been convened, given the privilege and function, gift and task, to be pioneers in what God wills for the world. Their gatherings, their life together, their congregations, are called to model the meaning of life as social, revealed in Jesus as the Christ. They come together, are brought together, in order to risk, explore, and share graced reality. In their ways of gathering, styles of leadership, and patterns of worship they all receive from each other, as means of grace, so that what they are and do and become together expresses the reality of God among them.

> So, my dear brothers, what conclusion is to be drawn? At *all* your meetings, let *everyone* be ready with a psalm or a sermon or a revelation, or ready to use his gift of tongues or to give an interpretation; but it must *always* be for the *common* good. (I Cor. 14:26, JB; emphasis added)

Such enactments of shared grace, casting down the proud and exalting the lowly, and all the while sending shivers through all kinds of hierarchical mentalities, are simply re-hearsals of that promised and promising realm where only God rules by love. Assemblies which are genuinely Christian question, defy, and make questionable all artificial distinctions—whether of race, sex, or status (Gal. 3:28). Truly Christian assemblies are subversive, for in act and by example they subvert most ordinary patterns of leadership, as honored guests become waiters and waiters become honored guests (Luke 22:24–27). Furthermore, as the New Testament emphasis upon "hospitality" makes obvious, such an assembly flouts the normal patterns of associative behavior. It welcomes, is hospitable, indeed "loves the stranger."

Something of this rehearsal by assembly has characterized truly Christian assemblies from their beginnings; and the historian Peter Brown aptly recounts their significance in *The World of Late Antiquity:*

> The Church was also professedly egalitarian. A group in which there was "neither slave nor free" might strike an aristocrat as utopian, or subversive. Yet in an age when the barriers separating the successful freedman from the *déclassé* senator were increasingly unreal, a religious group could take the final step of ignoring them. In Rome the Christian community of the early third century was a place where just such anomalies were gathered and tolerated: the Church included a powerful freedman chamberlain of the emperor; its bishop was the former slave of that freedman; it was protected by the emperor's mistress, and patronized by noble ladies.
>
> For men whose confusions came partly from no longer feeling embedded in their home environment, the Christian Church offered a drastic experiment in social living, rein-

forced by the excitements and occasional perils of a break
with one's past and one's neighbours.[24]

And, in a world rigorously stratified and coming unglued,
such hospitable assemblies were rehearsals for the renewal of
society. When they are truly themselves, Christian assemblies are not closed societies, tightly shuttered against outsiders. Their windows and doors are open. Their boundaries
are permeable. They are gathered and gathering, for in their
welcomes they rehearse realizations of grace.

As Christians assemble they *proclaim.* By and in their
gatherings they recognize, enact, and announce what they
know of God's unitive purposes. Their congregations are
living testimonies to God's way with the world, celebrating
and sharing, through deed and word, the truth of graced
being together. Such assemblies model and bear witness to
the social character of reality. Indeed, as the Society of
Friends eloquently demonstrates, simply being together may
itself be a means of grace. For them, surely, "meeting" is the
sacrament, even though worship is often silent and without
so-called sacraments; and such meetings are enacted parables and telling symbols of God's presence among people in
the world. Gatherings of Christians are signs that proclaim
the promised gathering of all peoples within the purposes of
God. Simply by assembling, Christians testify to the reality
in their midst; and in gathering, in the primordial act of
worship as meeting, in graced and gracious assembly, where
all are engaged and where strangers are genuinely welcomed,
reality may disclose promising secrets. In reality, since earliest Christian times, such gatherings are themselves acts of
evangelism, prompting the amazed recognition that "God
is really among you."

Chapter
III

THE LORD'S DAY

"The day Yahweh acted"

What hath this day deserv'd? What hath it done,
That it in golden letters should be set
Among the high tides in the calendar?
                    —Shakespeare, *King John*

From Yahweh this has come to pass,
    it is wondrous in our eyes.
This is the day Yahweh acted,
    let us exult and rejoice in him!
                    —Psalm 118:23–24,
                        The Anchor Bible

But if the horoscope's
    bewildering
. . . .
Who can turn skies back and begin again?
                    —Benjamin Britten,
                        Peter Grimes

Those who had walked in ancient practices at-
tained unto newness of hope, no longer observing
sabbaths but fashioning their lives after the Lord's
day, on which our life also arose through Him.
                    —Ignatius of Antioch,
                        To the Magnesians

"The day Yahweh acted"

Time is the fundamental environment of human consciousness. Humans are born, live, dream, suffer, and die in time.
The relentless impact of time is built into our tissues. Time
heals and time is cruel. Time is the realm of continuity and
change, of repetition and novelty. We experience time as
repetition while day follows day; we experience time as novelty when day shades into night, night brightens into day,
as the moon waxes and wanes, or as winter blossoms into
spring. Across the world, from earliest times, humans seem
to have found ways of marking time; and their calendars
have fixed upon the rotation of the earth on its axis, the
orbital motion of the moon about the earth, or the orbital
motion of the earth about the sun. Hence, the fundamental
units have been days, months, seasons, and years; and, as the
anthropologists remind us, every known culture appears to
take some note of time, as people live their lives according
to some scheme of time.

The marking of time gives pattern to life, setting se-
quences of activities, duties, and delights. Our lives are measured by years, we make appointments in hours and minutes,
and birthdays and anniversaries prompt times of festivity
and give meaning to our days. Measured time punctuates
life, interjecting commas, periods, question marks, and ex-
clamation points into the pulses and rhythms of the everyday. Of course, novelty without repetition is frantic, but

repetition without novelty is tiresome; and, as Plato knew, holidays "provide relief from this fatigue."[25] Festivals may be windows in time, opening our lives to the truly momentous. Or festivals may simply furnish diversion and respite from ennui; or they may fill our time with symbolic power. They may be solemn or they may be frivolous, but they are not ordinary. People dress up or down, they feast or fast, and they engage in distinctive behavior.

The celebration of time re-creates meaning in human life. The ancient Romans knew this surely, as they patterned their weeks to honor the planets, thereby giving cosmological import to time. Their days ran: (Dies) Saturni, Solis, Lunae, Martis, Mercurii, Jovis, and Veneris. Their times were patterned to give the heavenly bodies their due; and their pattern is reflected in the Saxon usage: Sun's Day, Moon's Day, Tiw's Day, Woden's Day, Thor's Day, Frigg's Day, and Saterne's Day. Interestingly enough, modern secular usage, begins not with the Dies Saturni of Rome or the Sun's Day of the Saxons, but with Monday:

> Monday's child is fair of face,
> Tuesday's child is full of grace,
> Wednesday's child is loving and giving,
> Thursday's child works hard for a living,
> Friday's child is full of woe,
> Saturday's child has far to go,
> But the child that is born on the Sabbath day
> Is brave and bonny, and good and gay.

Airline schedules, it may be noted, prosaically number their days, beginning with a businesslike number one (on Mondays) and working through the week to sixes and sevens, when business slows down. Thus even calendars and schedules, the observing or the marking of time, express—often unconsciously—understandings of reality.

I. The seven-day week is a legacy of Israel. Its core is a seventh day of rest after six days of work; and its origins lie hidden among the unsolved mysteries of ancient times. Scholars have suggested and espoused ingenious theories of its derivation from other cultures, whether Babylonian, Canaanite, or Kenite. They have sought a convincing etymology for the word "Sabbath," relating it to seven, or rest, or both; and they have sought to locate the origins of the seven-day week in the phases of the moon, a custom of periodic market days, or in the symbolic powers of the number seven—though that, of course, is simply to shift the problem from days to numbers! Whence comes the symbolic power of seven?

In any event, the ancient Hebrews appear simply to have counted and numbered their days, with little regard for the phases of the moon or the positions and movements of the planets. For us, at least, seven is arbitrary. It represents a free ordering of time, not bound by natural cycles. In its own way, it is quite unnatural. Israel's fundamental rhythm—the week with its culminating sabbath—was not linked to the seasons. Although Israel had its seasonal festivals, its basic celebration was of the sabbath; and, for Israel, the sabbath was rooted simply in the mysterious but nonetheless sure logic of divine command. Hence, what mattered was not natural rhythm or human moods but the divine mandate. For Israel, humanity had not shaped the Sabbath, but humanity was to be shaped by it. The Sabbath patterned and symbolized life, giving it pulse and purpose. The days ascended, like steps going up to Jerusalem. The days ascended, by number, one through five, to the sixth of preparation and the seventh of Sabbath, with each day beginning at sunset.

In ancient Israel the Sabbath was a given, with its own intrinsic logic, requiring no external validation. It was simply commanded that Israel rest every seventh day. Nevertheless, during the course of Israel's history, the institution was given various rationales. It was early understood on humanitarian grounds: "Six days you shall do your work, but on the seventh day you shall rest; that your ox and your ass may have rest, and the son of your bondmaid, and the alien, may be refreshed" (Ex. 23:12). Later, in the Priestly tradition, the seventh day was called the "Sabbath," and it was given a cosmic validity. It was grounded in the Creator's rest after six days of creation, "for in six days the LORD made heaven and earth, the sea, and all that is in them, and rested the seventh day; therefore the Lord blessed the sabbath day and hallowed it" (Ex. 20:11). In the Priestly tradition, the Sabbath is the pause that refreshes, the time when God rested and was refreshed. As such, it is a "sign" between God and Israel (Ex. 31:17). Meanwhile, the Deuteronomic tradition grounded the Sabbath in the exodus: "You shall remember that you were a servant in the land of Egypt, and the LORD your God brought you out thence with a mighty hand and an outstretched arm; therefore the LORD your God commanded you to keep the sabbath day" (Deut. 5:15). Later, in the Holiness Code, the Sabbath has become a religious festival. The day of rest has become the occasion for assemblies: "Six days shall work be done; but on the seventh day is a sabbath of solemn rest, a holy convocation; you shall do no work; it is a sabbath to the LORD in all your dwellings" (Lev. 23:3). In the traditions of Israel, the seventh day is the day of rest, a Sabbath, a holy day, a day of assembly; and its rationales unite humanitarian, cosmic, covenantal, and cultic concerns.

In a profound sense, the Sabbath is the definitive symbol of Israel's reality. Rooted in the covenant, it makes the calendar itself a living reminder of the exodus. Rooted in the creation, it hallows time. According to the Priestly story of creation in Genesis, God creates creatures and declares them good; God creates humans and blesses them; but only the seventh day is blessed and made holy. According to the Priestly reading of creation, the Sabbath surpasses not only all the other days but even humans in holiness. The Sabbath is the sign of God's freedom. God is not bound by the powers and forces, cycles and seasons, of the cosmos. God is free to rest and remain God even while resting. The Sabbath is not simply the sign of Israel; it is Israel's testimony to the very goodness of God. In the Sabbath, according to Israel, holiness is revealed, not only in time but as time. Because God so chooses, time itself is holy.

No wonder that among the Jews the Sabbath became *the* commandment, perhaps surpassing all others. Since God celebrated the Sabbath, to honor the Sabbath was to participate in God's celestial solemnities. As God's creatures, humans were created for God, and they live out their destiny by living for the Sabbath.

> If you cease to tread the sabbath underfoot,
> and keep my holy day free from your own affairs,
> if you call the sabbath a day of joy
>   and the LORD's holy day a day to be honoured,
>   if you honour it by not plying your trade,
>   not seeking your own interest
>   or attending to your own affairs,
> then you shall find your joy in the LORD,

and I will set you riding on the heights of the earth,
and your father Jacob's patrimony shall be yours to enjoy;
the LORD himself has spoken it.

(Isa. 58:13–14, NEB)

Thus, as it was put in a rabbinic midrash on Exodus, "If Israel keeps one Sabbath as it should be kept, the Messiah will come. The Sabbath is equal to all the other precepts of the Torah."[26] For devout Jews, the days are lived for the Sabbath. They are steps of ascent to the summit. The Sabbath is their culmination and crown. Its rationale is no longer to provide respite from labors, so that people may return to their work restored; instead, in the words of the saintly Abraham Joshua Heschel, "The Sabbath is not for the sake of the weekdays; the weekdays are for the sake of Sabbath. It is not an interlude but the climax of living."[27] In many ways, as a sanctuary in time, the Sabbath marks the summit of the piety of Judaism.

II. Jesus of Nazareth was a Jew, reared in a culture within which Sabbath observance was commonplace. Rabbinic law was filled with intricate prescriptions for proper resting on the Sabbath; and the sabbath had become the day for assembly in the synagogues. It was the time and place for the learning and teaching of Torah. Therefore, the Synoptic Gospels report not only that Jesus "went to the synagogue, as his custom was, on the sabbath day" (Luke 4:16) but that much of his teaching was done in the synagogue on the Sabbath. Indeed, according to Luke 4:16–30, Jesus encountered his first opposition as he taught on the Sabbath in the synagogue at Nazareth.

Throughout the Gospels, Jesus is busy on the Sabbath. He not only teaches; he also heals. He heals the crippled, the lame, and the blind. According to the Synoptic Gospels, Jesus provokes the Pharisees by healing a man with a withered hand on the Sabbath in the synagogue (Matt. 12:9–14; Mark 3:1–6; Luke 6:6–11)! Of course, as the Gospels indicate, rabbinic teaching allowed for works of necessity, whether ceremonial or humane, on the Sabbath. It was, for example, required to circumcise on the eighth day, even if that were the Sabbath; and it was permissible to rescue endangered animals; and medical treatment was allowed when life was endangered. But Jesus' Sabbath works were an affront. At their heart, they were works of mercy, not of necessity. In every case reported, the healing could doubtless have been postponed. Nevertheless, because humans are precious, more precious than the law, Jesus transforms the sabbath from a day of rest to a day of rescue. What was the exception becomes the rule. "Clearly, good deeds may be performed on the sabbath" (Matt. 12:12, NAB). In the ministry of Jesus, the Sabbath becomes the exemplary day for restoring humanity to wholeness. It gives occasion for those works in which God delights. According to the Gospels, Jesus' actions on the Sabbath not only are signs of his mission but also furnish opportunities for him to announce what he is about. When his disciples pluck grain on the Sabbath, he not only defends them but announces, "The sabbath was made for man, not man for the sabbath; so the Son of man is lord even of the sabbath" (Mark 2:27–28). And, according to John, when Jesus was criticized for healing on the Sabbath, he responded by saying, "My Father is working still, and I am working" (John 5:17).

Judaism had rooted its worship in the Sabbath, the day of rest. Holy rest was the climax of the week, and the

preparation for the Sabbath rest lent direction and meaning
to the works and workings of the week. The earliest Christians were Jews, most of them, nurtured in the seven-day
week of Judaism. Yet for them a decisive new event had
taken place, the event of the resurrection of Jesus; and it,
more than anything else, rearranged their whole vision of
reality. Even their sense of time! The early Christians re-
tained the seven-day week, with its numbering from one to
seven; but quite early, perhaps even in New Testament
times, they came to shift the emphasis from the seventh to
the first day. Thus in the four Gospels, documents where
every word seems chosen to count, the women visit the
tomb "on the first day of the week" (Matt. 28:1; Mark 16:2;
Luke 24:1; John 20:1). The disciples are gathered together
that night, the evening of "the first day of the week," and
are gathered together again "eight days later" (John 20:19,
26). Paul counsels the Corinthians to set aside contributions
on "the first day of every week" (I Cor. 16:2); and, in Troas,
Paul speaks "on the first day of the week, when we were
gathered together to break bread" (Acts 20:7). It appears,
especially since so few days are mentioned specifically in the
New Testament, that the first day is becoming the day for
the assembly. While not yet, perhaps, being called the
"Lord's day" (Rev. 1:10), it seems clear that the first day,
the day of resurrection, and the day of assembly are beginning to coincide, even within New Testament times.

III.   Although it is not clear in just what ways and to
what extent the earliest Christians related Sabbath and
Lord's Day, by the time of the apostolic fathers the Lord's
Day came to replace the Sabbath. It became *the* day of

assembly, with Christians gathering to *celebrate* their faith in their risen Lord. Worship became their exemplary work, setting the pattern for all their days. As Ignatius of Antioch put it:

> Those who had walked in ancient practices attained unto newness of hope, no longer observing sabbaths but fashioning their lives after the Lord's day, on which our life also arose through Him.[28]

Lives are to be lived and shaped, not according to the Sabbath rest but according to the Lord's resurrection. Resurrection, not rest, becomes the norm. The week takes its pattern from its beginning anew in Jesus. Life and light, already closely related in the Gospel of John, are united in fitting symbolism for the day of the assembly. According to Justin Martyr:

> The Day of the Sun is the day on which we all gather in a common meeting, because it is the first day, the day on which God, changing darkness and matter, created the world; and it is the day on which Jesus Christ our Savior rose from the dead.[29]

Hence the shift from Sabbath to Lord's Day was not simply a change of day, leaving the old obligation of days unchanged. For, as Paul observed to the Colossians (Col. 2: 6–23), sacred diets and calendars have been nailed to the cross. We are no longer to be judged by them, since they were but a foreshadowing of the reality of Christ. For Christians, the celebration of the Lord's Day is not a duty but an opportunity. To understand otherwise is to miss the point, since the Lord's Day itself is a festival of freedom. The Lord's Day is a gift, not a task. In every sense of the word, it is a *given* day. Indeed, even to speak of "observing" the

Lord's Day is to relapse into a slavery to times and seasons. It may be noted, incidentally, that the Council of Nicaea, with a sure instinct for the symbolic potency of gesture, resolved that Christians are to stand, not kneel, for prayer on the Lord's Day. Kneeling was the posture of subjects, and Christians had been raised with Christ. Because of Christ they were free to stand before God. In the instructive word-play of the Greek theologians on *anastasis,* they were raised to stand. Thus, just as Israel had rested on the Sabbath and had reclined at the Passover feast as a sign of freedom, so —at least on the Lord's Day—Christians are to enjoy their new stature before God. This is "the day Yahweh acted"— acted definitively by raising Jesus; and in that resurrection Christians too have been raised. At their living heart, therefore, their gatherings are simply glad celebrations of that reality.

As Christians gather at the beginning of each week, their assemblies *acknowledge* their new life together. New Testament Christianity is suffused with this newness. Against the tired wisdom of Ecclesiastes that "there is nothing new under the sun," it welcomes the new as God's work. The God whom the prophets knew as "doing a new thing" (Isa. 43:19), as creating "new heavens and a new earth" (Isa. 65:17), as making a "new covenant" (Jer. 31:31), and putting a "new spirit within them" (Ezek. 11:19), has now acted by raising Jesus from the dead. In Jesus as risen, the genuinely new has been realized, once and for all. Hence the New Testament is replete with images of the "new" *(kainos):* new wine, new teaching, new garment, new commandment, new covenant, new creation, new man, new nature, new heavens and a new earth, new name, new Jerusalem, and new song—culminating in the vision of Rev. 21:5: "And he who sat upon the throne said, 'Behold, I make all things new.' " This newness is not simply a matter of *time,* new as opposed to old. It has a *quality* of difference. It is fresh, not tired; it blossoms with the remarkable. It is somehow better than the old. The authentically new is filled, fairly bursting, with novel possibilities.

Like the beginning of creation, the Lord's Day is the first day. It is the day on which God would accomplish new things among people. In this sense Calvin, for instance, understood the Lord's Day as a day of rest, for in it people are to surrender their confidence in their own achievements, thereby opening themselves to the workings of God. We cease from *our* labors, he says, and are gathered together, that *God* may work in us. What mattered to Calvin was not a Sabbath rest, nor a vacation from responsibilities, but an occasion for gatherings genuinely open to God's grace. Hence, for Calvin, the day is truly the Lord's Day, to be spent with the Lord's people; and it is to be free from self-preoccupations, whether of labor or of leisure. This day, given as it is, provides opportunity for people to recognize God's works among them. In the words of Psalm 118:24, as paraphrased by Isaac Watts:

> This is the day the Lord hath made;
> He calls the hours his own;
> Let heaven rejoice, let earth be glad,
> And praise surround the throne.

As a new day, this day affords opportunity for a people and persons to begin life anew. On this day gatherings of Christians seek and find new resolve for their common life. Those who know themselves as the body of Christ in the world, risen from old and scattered ways into new and shared life, receive this day as an opportunity for the discovery of relationships, for the nurturing of bonds of affection, and for the devising of ventures in helpfulness and the restructuring of life together. This day is an open door, giving ample time and occasion to begin afresh, as people acknowledge new life among themselves and in each of them.

In a world of fates and furies, sin and guilt, estrangement and despair, the resurrection breathes hope; and even now, just as in the tired world of antiquity, the very possibility of conversion comes as a gracious surprise. The Lord's Day celebrates renewal, a letting go of the past with all its wrongs, hurts, and bondage. In Benjamin Britten's opera, the bewildered and tormented fisherman Peter Grimes asks, "Who can turn skies back and begin again?" And, unlike another and distant fisherman named Peter, he resists the grace offered by those who would befriend him, and he remains isolated in his estrangement. He simply will not let go. He remains closed to the grace of those who keep dreaming of what he might be. He resists those who keep reaching out for him. Stubbornly he persists in evil, as his dim past darkens his present and eclipses his future.

Among Christians, life is graced as together they live their days between resurrection and consummation. Their lives have a certain directionality as they are oriented, not toward the east, but toward the future. The Lord's Day is their source and summit. Time, not space, is the dominant category of their lives. Thus, with a felicitous ambiguity, the "Lord's Day" (Rev. 1:10) is the day for visions of God's triumph and it is an instance of the future in the present. It is a day alive with expectancy. As Basil of Caesarea puts it, on the day of the resurrection we stand for prayer, thus commemorating the grace given us, not only because we have been raised with Christ to seek the things which are above, but because "this day seems somehow an image of the expected age to come."[30] Like the prophetic "Day of the Lord," it is the final goal of history now impacting upon the present. In God's world, a world historical through and through, life is finally shaped by its ultimate direction and goal. To celebrate the Lord's Day is to acknowledge that life originates, is renewed, and culminates with God.

As Christians gather at the beginning of each week, their assemblies *rehearse* their new life together. In celebration of God's activity, they are summoned to act. This is the day for liturgy *(leitourgia),* the truly public work of God's people. On this day, their initial work is one of assembly, being gathered together (Acts 20:7). Their meetings are acts of assembly. The New Testament image of the body of Christ is vital. The body needs to be assembled in order to function. Some may be hands and some may be legs, but no member functions truly alone. Nevertheless, as Paul knew only too well, while hands may easily enjoy clasping hands with other hands, it is often difficult to get the whole body assembled and working together. The barriers of racism, classism, and sexism do not crumble easily—even though in Christ there is "neither Jew nor Greek, there is neither slave nor free, there is neither male nor female" (Gal. 3:28). True gatherings for worship require much openness and effort, as Christians let themselves be gathered across those embattled lines which still divide humanity.

Thus genuine assemblies on the Lord's Day are rehearsals of human interdependence, where Christians meet to try out, to act out, to learn to love and live with, life as it is meant to be. For this reason, throughout earliest Christianity, the "collection" had a profound theological significance. It was the offering that enacted interdependence. For example, in I Cor. 16:2, Paul enjoins the Corinthians: "On the first day of every week, each of you is to put something aside and store it up, as he may prosper." And in Paul's letters the word *koinōnia* means both community and contribution. There is no community without cost! The Lord's Day is the day to rehearse concrete interdependence through sharing. In the new covenant there is no life without giving; and the service of the neighbor honors God. "Each one, as a good manager of God's different gifts, must use for the good of others the special gift he has received from God" (I Peter 4:10, TEV). Here worship and service are so intertwined that the old and easy lines between sacred and secular lose their significance. Hence, work and worship are not antithetical but conjoined; and the Lord's Day offers an occasion for the doing of exemplary works.

The Lord's Day is truly celebrated when worship, work, and play are restored, if only for a moment, to their integral unity. Unfortunately, in our estranged world, they are usually defined by contrasts between them. They are wrenched apart, twisted and sundered; and life, in consequence, is often confused and sometimes tragically warped. Worship is often imagined apart from the concreteness of work; and work is often so dehumanizing that those who do not literally bury themselves in it seek meanings apart from it in the vagaries of diversions, pastimes, and vacations. Life itself disintegrates as liturgy, labor, and leisure are separated and skewed. Under such conditions, there is no true humanity, as worship becomes ethereal, work becomes onerous, and play becomes trifling.

However, as Rev. 1:10 suggests, the Lord's Day is the day for visions. Unlike other days, this day is not simply determined by the pressures of the past nor limited by the prospects of the present. It is the day when the consummation commences; it is the day given to be devoted to the rehearsal of behavior fit for the promised fulfillment of life. On the

Lord's Day, at least, God's people are already free from the entrenched answers of custom and the stifling questions of practicality. Those who pray for God's reign, kingdom, and will are graced—liberated and empowered—to rehearse God's triumph over sin and death. Above all days, this day is to be devoted to the dreaming together of uncommon dreams, for becoming suited to the matched garments of grace, gladness, and generosity, and for venturing to the very margins of humanizing possibilities. Incidentally, such a rehearsal is tellingly described in one of Martin Buber's tales of the Hasidim. A rabbi recounts that his grandfather was paralyzed. One day, when the grandfather was asked to tell about his pious teacher, the great Baal Shem, he told how the great rabbi used to leap about and dance while he prayed. Caught up in the ecstasy of the story, the grandfather began to demonstrate what the teacher had done, praying and dancing, and the old man was cured in the process.[31]

As Christians gather at the beginning of each week, their assemblies *proclaim* their new life together. What they do tells the secret of their lives, the good news of the gospel. In the words of Isaac Watts:

> Today the saints his triumph spread,
> And all his wonders tell.

In several languages—such as French, Greek, Italian, Russian, and Spanish—the names of the days commence with the Lord's Day. The impact of Christianity has been felt throughout many cultures, sometimes even leading to various forms of Sunday legislation. However, the definitive proclamations of this day continue to be those exemplary gatherings of Christians where diverse races, classes, and sexes meet in common life, honoring God and caring for the world. Such meetings proclaim by their very happening the surprising grace of the God who wills, creates, and restores a new humanity. Authentic Lord's Day assemblies are a *sign* to the world that, even if only momentarily, the future has already dawned. Indeed, in a world sundered by strife, where diaspora seems to rule, such graced gatherings are enacted parables of God's purpose to gather all humanity into one. Their mission to the world, as celebrated on the Lord's Day, is not Sabbath but shalom, not rest but peace. Thus, on the Lord's Day, acknowledging and rehearsing hopes nurtured by the resurrection, Christians gather; and their very gatherings, and what they do together at least on this day, are testimonies and celebrations of "the day Yahweh acted."

Chapter
IV

THE LORD'S FEAST

"As they were eating"

And as they were eating, he took bread, and
blessed, and broke it, and gave it to them.
—Mark 14:22a

On the Lord's day of the Lord, come together,
break bread, and give thanks.
—Didache 14:1

The Thanksgiving meal in expectation of the coming of the Kingdom is the only service of worship
in the earliest period. Purely preaching services are
unknown at this time. All prayer, prophecy and
teaching take place during the celebration of the
meal.
—Albert Schweitzer,
*The Kingdom of God
and Primitive
Christianity*

In the eucharist we christians concentrate our mo-
tive and act out our theory of human living.
—Gregory Dix,
*The Shape of the
Liturgy*

"As they were eating"

Worship, like work and play, is basically something to be done, not merely talked about. Anyone who has ever tried to read recipes for baking bread knows that there is finally no real substitute for mixing, kneading, and baking; and anyone who has ever tried to master the intricacies of chess knows that playing it, however clumsily, is far more illuminating than talking about it. And every lover knows that all the poems and treatises about lovemaking are simply tedious facts or dancing shadows compared with making love. For embodied creatures, reality lives, it works and plays, in enactment.

Hence, from ancient times, among Greeks and Romans, Jews and Christians, there has been a remarkable kinship between worship and drama. As Ivor Brown puts it, "Drama begins with action and spectacle; the deed comes before the word, the dance before the dialogue, the play of body before the play of mind."[32] Something of this is true in Plato's *Symposium*, where a drinking party gives Socrates occasion for a profound discussion of the meaning of love. This is certainly true in the celebration of the Jewish Passover, where it is the drama of sharing a meal which affords the occasion for dialogue about the meaning of existence. The meal is the indispensable foundation of the celebration; and the act of feasting itself gives food for thought. The Seder ("program") is a banquet for which the Haggadah ("recital") is the libretto. What is done is the basis for what is said. As at any truly festive event, the meal is accompanied by blessings, talk, and song. God is blessed for the gifts of food and drink, there is conversation about the significance of the occasion, and the festivities break into song. The meal itself matters; and the night of its celebration differs from all other nights. This festive night is the night for eating unleavened bread, for eating bitter herbs, for reclining, and for drinking at least four cups of wine. Each act has its meaning and is given its interpretation. The unleavened bread recalls the haste with which God saved Israel from Egypt; the bitter herbs recall the bitterness of slavery in Egypt; the reclining is a symbol of freedom, since slaves stand and serve while the free rest and enjoy; and no one, no matter how poor, is to be deprived of wine, of glad participation in the banquet of the redeemed. During Passover, within the program of a meal including bread and wine, the participants enact who they are, recite the ancient faith (Deut. 26:5–8), sing the Hallel (Psalms 113–118), and regard themselves as coming forth out of Egypt, from bondage into freedom.

Among Christians, Luke gives testimony to the power of the dramatic deed in his account of the journey to Emmaus (Luke 24:13–35). The risen Jesus meets two of his disciples on the road, and they discuss what has happened. They do not recognize him, even though he gives a good account of himself by interpreting the Scriptures. When they arrive at Emmaus, the disciples invite him to stay with them, to be their guest. Only then, at table, do they recognize him. Luke is speaking, surely, to the human fact that sharing a meal with someone is itself revelatory; but, even more decisively, this guest has played host. He, not one of his hosts, breaks the bread! In that, his characteristic gesture of giving, Jesus gave himself away. All that he had said to them on the road came into focus as "he was known to them in the breaking of the bread." A telling gesture spoke volumes; a meal shared revealed his reality. Because the Lord was present, ordinary bread served as his gift of himself to his disciples; it became his means of disclosure, and they recognized themselves as guests of his grace.

I.   Authentic Christian worship is grounded in the universal biological realities of hunger and thirst. No matter how refined its liturgies or elaborate its rubrics, it is rooted in the rudiments of animal necessity. Eating and drinking are the simplest requisites for survival. Like sparrows and turtles, cats and horses, humans must feed or be fed in order to live. No needs are simpler. Indeed, in most climates, clothes and shelter are sheer luxuries compared to the need for food and drink; and starvation is the cruelest form of neglect. Satisfying hunger and quenching thirst are perhaps the most natural activities; and, etymologically, even the most elegant *restaurant* can only disguise the fact that its irreducible functions are alimental, to *restore* the bodies of the famished. Furthermore, in cultures where resources are squandered in overindulgence in food and drink, obesity only obscures the common reality that humans everywhere must eat and drink or they die.

Nevertheless, as social anthropologist Mary Douglas reminds us, "food is not feed."[33] Eating and drinking are not simply biological occurrences. They are human occasions. Practical in origin, they are expressive in performance. Natural needs for nourishment are culturally refined through customs and patterns of behavior. Humans cook, compose

menus, and use utensils. They become mannered, as their
eating and drinking enact tacit commitments to a particular
people and to its ways of behaving. Humans break bread
together. Perhaps commensality is the primal venture of
sociality. Sharing food represents the basic conquest of humanity over animality. Hence to treat food as feed, thereby
rejecting the human dimensions of meals, is to "make a pig
of oneself." Those who eat hastily, indifferent to those about
them, are said to "wolf down their food." Incidentally,
something of this insight into the distinctively human is
captured in the Jewish wisdom literature:

> Do not reach out your hand for everything you see,
>   and do not crowd your neighbor at the dish.
> Judge your neighbor's feelings by your own,
>   and in every matter be thoughtful.
> Eat like a human being what is set before you,
>   and do not chew greedily, lest you be hated.
>   (Ecclus. 31:14–16)

In a hungry world, with scarcely enough to go around, manners are never simply manners. Table manners, as Claude
Lévi-Strauss and others have abundantly shown, express a
vision of reality.

Furthermore, the root metaphor of sociality, of
cohumanity, is companionship. Companionship, from *cum*
+ *panis*, "breading together," is a distinctively human activity, and is the essence of community. Shared meals, when
taken together by choice, do express human relationships.
Animals grab a hunk of meat and scamper off to gnaw on
it by themselves, or animals crowd each other in the trough;
while in virtually every culture, humans congregate compan-
ionately to eat. Eating and drinking are not simply biological
activities. They express the very texture of human associa-

tion. Sharing a meal is a vital symbol of social solidarity.
Meals express relationships; and they also constitute them.
As the French sociologist Émile Durkheim noted:

> In a multitude of societies, meals taken in common are be-
> lieved to create a bond of artificial kinship between those who
> assist at them. In fact, relatives are people who are naturally
> made of the same flesh and blood. But food is constantly
> remaking the substance of the organism. So a common food
> may produce the same effects as a common origin.[34]

Or, as Samuel Pepys told his diary, "Strange to see how a
good dinner and feasting reconciles everybody."

Yet, perhaps precisely because meals do express and create persons, humans draw lines at their tables. Meals are
marked by boundaries. Eating and drinking are occasions for
rules and for decisions. Except under the most extreme
circumstances, there are arbitrary limits to what anyone will
eat. Children sometimes draw the line at spinach, vegetari-
ans avoid meat, some people refuse shellfish or pork, snakes
or eel, horsemeat or roast dog; and most humans are revolted
by the thought of cannibalism. Eating and drinking are
natural processes, inevitably violent but natural; while diet,
the choice of food and drink, is a cultural fact. Society
directs and determines our acceptable sources of nutriment.
There are dietary boundaries. Meals are also marked by
social boundaries. Just as we do not always eat the most
accessible foodstuffs, so we do not always eat with the most
available neighbors. Decisions about whom we will eat with
are as real as decisions about what we will eat. Patterns of
commensality, "table-sharing," reveal many of the operative
structures of society. As Mary Douglas has observed in her
provocative study of English middle-class meal customs,
"Deciphering a Meal":

Drinks are for strangers, acquaintances, workmen, and family. Meals are for family, close friends, honored guests. The grand operator of the system is the line between intimacy and distance. Those we know at meals we also know at drinks. The meal expresses close friendship. Those we know only at drinks we know less intimately.[35]

Food is not simply feed; and meals are social realities of immense import. Thus the social force of excommunication resides in its refusal of commensality. When we refuse to share a meal with people, their humanity is impugned, spurned, or denied. As humans set boundaries to their tables, their tables often become refuges for racism, sexism, classism, and pharisaism. Indeed, with graceful power or pernicious force, meals enact profound social realities.

Feed shared by humans is food, furnishing more than nutrition; and food eaten in celebration of someone or something, some person or event, is a feast. Feasts are shared meals with festivities. The food and drink may be sumptuous; but the occasion is made festive by the measure of conviviality. Lavish buffets are not enough to make a feast. Feasts are social occasions where people open themselves to one another, become truly vulnerable to one another, and nurture one another in liveliness. Hence even our language about feasts is exuberant. We feed ourselves, we serve or share food, and we give banquets or give dinners—but feasts are parties, and you "throw parties"!

Feasts often include eating and drinking, talking, singing, and dancing. At their best, feasts afford genuine opportunities for human communion, for giving and receiving. They enact what human life is all about. The food may be simple bread, wine, and good talk, or it may be the fragile cake, effervescent champagne, and joyous toasts of a wedding; but whatever the fare, feasts are occasions for eating, drinking, and conversing. Feasts are events of human communion, where life itself is spirited and thereby somehow hallowed. As such, all true feasts are ecstatic. Feasts are ultimately trysts with transcendence, since all glad communion is eucharistic. Something of this is suggested in the savory words of the poet Octavio Paz:

> The eucharist is a mystery that is present in all our rituals, whether religious or erotic. The two most beautiful and meaningful images that tradition has passed down to us are the Platonic symposium and Christ's Last Supper. In both, wine is a cardinal symbol whereby our civilization defines its dual vocation; it is the archetype of communication—with others and with the Other.[36]

Incidentally, the English language offers remarkable testimony to this intricate relation between worship and food. The crucial term "lord," filled as it is with theological, social, and political overtones, is derived from loaf + ward, "keeper of bread." A lord is one upon whom you depend for sustenance, life given in a meal.

II.   From beginning to end, the Bible is interested in food and drink. Its story begins in a garden and ends in a city; and while there are no temples in the garden of Eden or in the new Jerusalem, both have fruit trees and streams of water. Whether in the temptation of fruit or in the promise of feast, meals in the Bible are replete with reality and are vital testimonies to divine activity, presence, and purpose. Since food and drink nurture and restore life, they are exemplary gifts of God's care. The wanderers in the wilderness are given manna and water; and the psalmist tells of God as one who provides a meal, indeed a bounteous feast with a spread of food, festive oil on the faces of the guests, and drink flowing freely:

> You prepare a table before me
>   under the eyes of my enemies;
> you anoint my head with oil,
>   my cup brims over.
>   (Ps. 23:5, JB)

Indeed, it is God who waters the plants from which humans get

> wine to make them cheerful,
> oil to make them happy
> and bread to make them strong.
>   (Ps. 104:15, JB)

The imagery is festive. God gives strength and delight.

Feasts are crucial in the life and history of Israel. In the epic of the exodus, Moses and Aaron begin their dealings with Pharaoh with the words, "Thus says the Lord, the God of Israel, 'Let my people go, that they may hold a feast to me in the wilderness'" (Ex. 5:1). They ask for only three days' leave, a minor deliverance; but their purpose is a feast. The pattern is set. Deliverance is to be celebrated in feasting before God. Furthermore, the covenant—God's treaty with Israel—is ratified in activities that culminate in a meal. Moses and the leaders of Israel "beheld God, and ate and drank" (Ex. 24:11b). Israel celebrates great moments with feasting. The ceremonies for the enthronements of Solomon as king, for example, include a feast. "They ate and drank that day in Yahweh's presence with great joy" (I Chron. 29:22, JB). Such meals are not aimless riots of mirth. Their integrity rests in the dedicated enthusiasm with which the people receive the gifts of covenant or leadership and oblige themselves to live out their promises. The feasts of the covenanted have ethical import. Those who genuinely know themselves as created, restored, and freed in feasts live Job's recognition (Job 31:17) that eating alone, refusing to share with the hungry, is a sin. Throughout the Bible, worship, feasts, and social justice are integrally related. Hence the people of the covenants, old and new, look to the time when all will have their due share of food and drink. The prophets dream of feasts yet to come. According to Isaiah,

> On this mountain the LORD of Hosts will prepare
> a banquet of rich fare for all the peoples,
> a banquet of wines well matured and richest fare,
> well-matured wines strained clear.
>
> (Isa. 25:6, NEB)

And Jesus tells of the messianic banquet: "Many, I tell you, will come from east and west to feast with Abraham, Isaac, and Jacob in the kingdom of Heaven" (Matt. 8:11, NEB). The image used for feasting, here as elsewhere, is reclining, the eating and drinking posture of free people. Finally, the consummation of history is mirrored in a meal, where the generations of humanity are free to relax together as at a feast. And, in an image that marries a multitude of biblical themes, the final triumph is realized in the ultimate banquet of banquets: "Happy are those who are invited to the wedding feast of the Lamb" (Rev. 19:9, JB).

Like the feasts of ancient Greece and Rome, the feasts of the Bible are filled with food and drink, talk and song, and sometimes even dancing. They are occasions for rejoicing. They are celebrations of reality. Yet, no matter how static or ecstatic their character, or how frugal or lavish their fare,

or how silent or talkative the guests, the meals of the Bible
are received, almost without exception, as religious occasions. They offer humans an opportunity to recognize God.
As the Talmud quotes Rabbi Akiba, "A man is forbidden to
taste anything before saying a blessing over it" (Berakoth
6:35a). When God is blessed for food and drink, every meal
becomes an act of worship. The blessing is an acknowledgment of God. In what may really be their most authentic
difference from the rest of the animals, humans bless their
food and give thanks for it. Strictly speaking, of course, it
is God who is blessed, not the food. Food and drink, like
men and women, need no hallowing. They were hallowed
as they came from the hands of God. As Gustaf Dalman
observes:

> It is in any case to be borne in mind that it is not the elements
> of food and drink that were blest; these are not changed by
> the blessing into something new, to which the Divine now
> becomes somehow attached: the object of the benediction is
> God Himself, who is the Creator and Distributor of all good
> things. The relation between what is to be eaten or drunk and
> God consists in the fact that it comes from Him, and the
> significance of the blessing is just this, that before starting to
> eat and drink, the person recognises this fact.[37]

Thus, in the time of Jesus, *every* meal was an act of praise
as the breaking of bread commenced with the words of
blessing: "Blessed are you, Lord our God, King of the universe, who brings forth bread from the earth."[38] And, in the
time of Jesus, at the feasts, they all doubtless sang the Hallel
("Praise"), Psalms 113–118, including the lines

> I will lift up the cup of salvation
>   and call on the name of the LORD,
>
> . . . .

> I will offer to thee the sacrifice of thanksgiving
> and call on the name of the LORD.
>
> (Ps. 118:13, 17)

III. According to the four Gospels, Jesus eats and drinks. Only heretics and the thoughtless have ever doubted his need for nourishment. There is nothing unusual about a person who eats, or even about a rabbi who likes food and drink. Indeed, in the fascinating cookbook *A Taste of Heaven,* Lionel Blue remarks how "Jewish" the Gospels are because there is so much about eating:

> There was the marriage feast at Cana, dinner with Pharisees, catering for rallies, stories about fatted calves, the Last Supper of course, and my own favorite—the fried fish breakfast with the risen Christ at the lakeside described at the end of St. John's Gospel (I never quite understood the story but then neither apparently did the Gospel writer).[39]

What is remarkable in the Gospels is not the fact that Jesus eats and drinks but that so much attention is given to reporting that he does. His meals seem to be of such moment as to deserve special mention. There is something quite definitive about his eating and drinking. As mountains are defined by their height and lakes and streams are defined by their water, he is defined as someone who speaks in parables, heals people, and shares meals. In a word—for the Gospels, meals with Jesus are momentous events, worthy of comment and remembrance. Who he is, is revealed in the meals he shares. Meals are, so to speak, among his "means of grace." He graces the meals he attends. Often host, he is never simply guest. What matters is not his presence but his activity. He always gives more than he receives. Indeed, for the Gospels, he might be characterized as the one who shares feasts with sinners.

In the parable of the great banquet, told as table talk in Luke 14, Jesus explains his whole ministry. He is the servant of a Master who gives feasts.

> One of the men sitting at the table heard this and said to Jesus, "How happy are those who will sit at the table in the Kingdom of God!"
>
> Jesus said to him, "There was a man who was giving a great feast, to which he invited many people. At the time for the feast he sent his servant to tell his guests, 'Come, everything is ready!' But they all began, one after another, to make excuses. The first one told the servant, 'I bought a field, and have to go and look at it; please, accept my apologies.' Another one said, 'I bought five pairs of oxen and am on my way to try them out; please accept my apologies.' Another one said, 'I have just gotten married, and for this reason I cannot come.' The servant went back and told all this to his master. The master of the house was furious and said to his servant, 'Hurry out to the streets and alleys of the town, and bring back the poor, the crippled, the blind, and the lame.' Soon the servant said, 'Your order has been carried out, sir, but there is room for more.' So the master said to the servant, 'Go out to the country roads and lanes, and make people come in, so that my house will be full. I tell you all that none of those men who were invited will taste my dinner!' " (Luke 14:15–24, TEV)

This Jesus, the Jesus of the parable, eats and drinks. Unlike John the Baptist and his followers, Jesus and his disciples eat and drink so much as to cause comment. Far from being an ascetic recluse, Jesus is accused as "a glutton and a drunkard, a friend of tax collectors and sinners" (Matt. 11:19). In

Jericho he accepts hospitality from Zacchaeus, a tax collector, presumed to be a sinner (Luke 19:1–10). He enters the home of Levi, where he eats with many "sinners and tax collectors" (Mark 2:13–17). And, according to Luke:

> One time many tax collectors and outcasts came to listen to Jesus. The Pharisees and the teachers of the Law started grumbling, "This man welcomes outcasts and even eats with them!" (Luke 15:1–2, TEV)

Furthermore, Jesus not only welcomes the outcasts; he tells others to do the same. And, according to Luke 14:7–14, he not only counsels the guests on their manners at a wedding feast but even tells his host how to plan a party!

Wherever he goes, he seems bent upon overturning the customary patterns of propriety. At every meal, so to speak, he turns the tables. Invited as guest, he acts as host; as he receives hospitality, he presumes to offer it. In the feeding of the five thousand (Mark 6:32–44) and of the four thousand (Mark 8:1–10), for example, what is startling is not only the multiplication of the loaves and fish. What is amazing is the ease with which *he* says the blessing, thereby acting as host with the food others have provided. Even the Passover he celebrated with his disciples took place, according to Mark and Luke, in a "guest room." And at Emmaus the risen Jesus, invited to stay as guest, was recognized when, as host, "he took the bread and blessed, and broke it, and gave it to them" (Luke 24:30). Throughout the Gospels, Jesus is so surely identified as the giver of food and drink that, for his followers, every meal they share is animate with gestures of his self-giving.

Of all the meals of Jesus with his disciples, ecclesiastical tradition has tended to fix upon the last meal he shared with them before his death. This meal has been singled out, celebrated, and revered above all the others. There are obviously many reasons for this, and their several rationales have sparked many quarrels and filled many books. The studies of the few brief biblical passages which report that one meal have filled innumerable volumes. On this vast topic, surely no one can master the literature. However, it should not go unnoticed that much of this labor has not only distinguished but also separated this meal from all the others. Even the vigorous controversies as to whether this meal was actually a *Passover* meal have, unhappily, tended to overlook the fact that it was a *meal.* In effect, many scholarly discussions of this meal seem at times to resemble what might result if people who had never attended a wedding banquet tried to reconstruct and comprehend such an event when their only clues were promises at the cutting of the cake and a toast proposed at the raising of a glass. Consequently, in order for its true meaning to be glimpsed again, this meal needs to be restored to its own sumptuous and illuminating contexts of genuine meals, Jewish meal customs, and the evident import of Jesus' other reported meals. What so many seem to have missed for so long is precisely what the earliest Christians could so easily take for granted. For example, even Paul, that thorough theologian of the early church, whom no one would accuse of denigrating the "Lord's supper," was, after all, only moved to mention it because of the catastrophe at Corinth. At a distance, after centuries of tradition, it is sometimes difficult to realize how occasional many of the biblical documents are; and, except for the preservation of Paul's response to the scandalous conduct of the Christians at Corinth, scholars might freely argue that the earliest decades of Christianity knew nothing of a common meal shared in "remembrance" of Jesus. In any event, it should be recognized that in Paul's term "Lord's supper," the word *deipnon* (translated "supper") means feast, banquet, dinner, the main meal of the day—usually shared in the evening. It is, in fact, the word used by Luke in the parable of the great banquet.

The earliest account of the institution of the Lord's feast is probably that given by Paul in the context of his scolding of the Corinthians:

> For I received from the Lord what I also delivered to you, that the Lord Jesus on the night when he was betrayed took bread, and when he had given thanks, he broke it, and said, "This is my body which is for you. Do this in remembrance of me." In the same way also the cup, after supper, saying, "This cup is the new covenant in my blood. Do this, as often as you drink it, in remembrance of me." (I Cor. 11:23–25)

On the basis of what we know of New Testament times, how was this meal supposed to be different? What was new and distinctive about it? How, and in what ways, did it resemble other meals, whether festive or ordinary?

So far as we know, bread was basic to every Jewish meal. The Passover feast, for example, was distinctive because the bread was unleavened, not because bread was served. Bread was the basic food, serving even as the utensil with which to scoop up, and sop up, other foods. A meal without bread was no meal at all. Wine was more costly, and not so plentiful. Only the wealthy could afford it with frequency; others enjoyed it on special occasions. Hence, at the Passover feast, "even the poorest in Israel" must have at least four cups of wine. The cup is one of rejoicing, and drinking from it recalls God's saving covenant. Among the Jews, bread and wine were indispensable components in every festive meal. Bread was broken and a cup was passed as meals were shared gladly. Meals were sometimes called "the breaking of bread." Yet this meal was not distinctive because bread was broken or a cup shared. Among the Jews, it was customary for the head of a household, the host, to commence a meal, after blessing bread, by tearing the bread into pieces and sharing it. The act had no cultic significance; it was simply utilitarian and social. Since every true meal was a social occasion, sharing bread was an act of human solidarity. That it was done seemed natural; it deserved comment only as mention of who did it, since the blessing and breaking were hostly acts of hospitality. Furthermore, although the "Lord's supper" or "breaking of bread" came to be called the "eucharist" (thanksgiving), the distinctiveness of the meal did not reside in the blessings or thanksgivings. Among the Jews, to eat without praising God as the true giver of food was unthinkable. Prayer, therefore, was an indispensable component of every meal. No meal commenced or finished without it. The host spoke the blessing, since blessing constituted the meal as meal; though occasionally a guest might be asked to give the thanks (to God!) at the conclusion of the meal. Thus every meal was truly an act of worship, set in the context of the memory and promise of God's faithfulness to Israel.

Quite simply, what made this meal distinctive was that it, supremely, was the *Lord's* feast. It was perceived as a definitive act of Jesus' self-giving to his disciples. The interpretive words, as recounted by Paul, only serve to make this abundantly clear. Among the Jews, interpretive words were spoken at the Passover feast, telling the meaning of the unleavened bread, the bitter herbs, the lamb, and the reclining at table. The Passover meal recalls Israel to the exodus, so that those who share it regard themselves as if they themselves came forth out of Egypt. Here, in contrast, the words focus upon the one who shares the bread and the cup.

These are his gifts of himself, his gestures of generosity, to be received in recognition of him. There is, once its Jewish context is understood, nothing unique about this meal except that it occasions recognition of him. Hence every meal received in recognition of him shares something of this meal. As Gustaf Dalman puts it:

> To our Lord it did not, as we have seen, mean the institution of a new custom, but only the giving of a new significance to the old, which should from henceforth continually envisage Him in the midst of the Meal-fellowship of the Disciples.[40]

Nothing is different, and yet everything is, for everything now has a different and surpassing rationale. Eating and drinking now make sense in a new way. Because of Jesus, every meal becomes an occasion for joy. Acts reports of the earliest Christians that, "breaking bread in their homes, they partook of food with glad and generous hearts, praising God" (Acts 2:46–47). In the New Testament at least, if not always after, the message seems clear: *Among Christians, every meal with bread and wine, gratefully received and gladly shared, is the Lord's feast, insofar as Jesus is recognized in it.*

Parenthetically, if such is the New Testament's understanding of the Lord's feast, it was soon obscured as Christianity moved out from Jerusalem and was adapted to new situations. In the century from Paul to Justin Martyr, roughly from A.D. 50 to 150, at least three massive and momentous shifts took place: from meal to menu, from people to president, and from evening to morning gatherings for worship. Each of these shifts was significant. Taken together, the results were revolutionary. Meals became sacraments! Hence, although they can only be hinted at here, each of these moves deserves to be traced, analyzed, and pondered with care.

Paul testifies to a tradition of communal meals within which bread and cup were only moments. In Paul, and in the Gospels of Mark and Matthew, things happened "after supper" or "as they were eating." However, already in Corinth, the bread and the cup seem to have been brought together as a religious event following the common meal. The "eucharist," so to speak, follows the "agape." And that division, once made, is hard to heal, since it indicates a fatal split between secular and sacred, ordinary and sacramental. Hence, by the time of Justin, the word about the bread and the word about the cup, asymmetrical in Paul, have become symmetrical: "This is my body"; "This is my blood"—and the food has been somehow transformed by thanksgiving. It is "eucharistized," and may be transported, as sacred food, to those who are absent from the assembly—as if a piece of wedding cake were a plausible substitute for being at the wedding!

In Paul there is no mention of (or interest in?) who presides, since for him the meal is still basically the Lord's feast with his people. Perhaps whoever furnished his (or her?) home as a meeting place said the blessings over the meal, or perhaps all the people gathered recited the blessings together. In any event, as his words to the Corinthians make utterly clear, the solidarity of the *koinōnia,* with their Lord and with each other, was crucial. And in the Didache it is the people who are instructed to gather together, break bread, and give thanks. Their thanks are in the plural: "We give thanks to you, our Father"! In Justin, however, the bread and wine are brought to the "president," who takes them. He "offers prayers and thanksgivings to the best of his ability, and the people assent, saying the Amen" (*First Apol-*

ogy 67.5). The people are becoming secondary, not simply to their Lord but to a president (or priest?) who has the right (and power?) to confect sacred food and drink.

> On the first day of the week, when we were gathered together to break bread, Paul talked with them, intending to depart on the morrow; and he prolonged his speech until midnight. (Acts 20:7)

Paul and the earliest Christians gathered in the evening, and their prayers, conversation, and song were in the context of the major meal of the day. However, by the time of Justin, for whatever reasons (if reasons there were), their gatherings were on Sunday mornings. The pattern is no longer evening meal, including talk and song, or even meal followed by sacrament, but gatherings for "religious" purposes, with word followed by sacrament. A banquet with Christian dimensions has become a service of worship that retains some vestigial reminders of a sacred feast. By the way, it may be noted that what began as a banquet with after-dinner speeches and song has tended to become, among many Christians, religious assemblies that are mostly speech, little song, and no dinner! Along such lines, with or without "sacraments," worship tends to become separated from life. As it pretends to be spiritual, it loses all human sense, becoming ethereal and unreal. Thus, although something of the sharing that is so obvious in Acts 2:42–47 continues in Justin, where gifts are brought to the president who gives them to the needy, it is not far along the road of a feastless spirituality to a studied indifference to such mundane matters. For a sobering example of the danger, remember that strange rubric of the *Westminster Directory* of 1644 that "The Collection for the poore is so to be ordered, that no part of the publique worship be thereby hindred."

IV.   Eating and drinking together in recognition of
Jesus is the basic act of *acknowledgment* by Christians of
what God has done, is doing, and will do through him. As
acknowledgment, the emphasis is not first upon what we do
but upon what God does. Those who gather in recognition
of Jesus know themselves as guests, invited to the table.
What they bring is incidental, as incidental as the loaves and
fishes or the meal the disciples offered and Jesus hosted to
reveal himself at Emmaus. Ultimately, we have nothing real
to offer, nothing that really makes the difference. The real
difference, what really matters, is his hospitality. He is the
sharer, making our meals his feasts, occasions of his grace.
As such, meals are not basically our acts, whether of offering
or of thanksgiving. The Lord's feast is the *Lord's* feast; it
is a means of his graciousness, as we acknowledge him.

Eating and drinking together in recognition of Jesus is the
basic act of *rehearsal* by Christians of what life is all about.
As rehearsal, the emphasis is upon acting out, tasting the
future toward which God is drawing all human reality. As
Paul knew well, and as the anthropologists remind us, sharing meals, commensality, is a political act. To share a table
acknowledges the humanity of those with whom one shares
it; to refuse to share is a repudiation of the other. Thus, in
what may be the earliest theology of the Lord's feast, Paul
writes: "Because there is one loaf, we, many as we are, are
one body; for it is one loaf of which we all partake" (I Cor.
10:17, NEB). Those who are already somehow related eat
together as a matter of course. Their common meals simply
enact their relationships. But meals also create relationships.
That is their grace. It makes them troublesome and creative,

for those who eat together are, like it or not, somehow bound together. Hence, meals are risky affairs, for they open people to relationships they may never have dreamt of having. No wonder the racial integration of restaurants has been so difficult; and, perhaps, no wonder that Christians have done almost everything, it seems, to keep their worship from being anchored in a genuine meal. No wonder! Even their tables, such as they are, have often been scrupulously fenced against the unwanted. Jesus, obviously, knew the power of meals, so he shared them gladly, graciously using them to question and erode the various boundaries religion and society had erected between people. As a rehearsal, the Lord's feast enacts something of realities yet to come. This meal is to be shared in expectation; it is a foretaste yearning for fulfillment. In the words of the Didache:

> As this broken bread was scattered over the mountains and when brought together became one, so let your Church be brought together from the ends of the earth into your kingdom.

Eating and drinking together in recognition of Jesus is the basic act of *proclamation* by Christians. "For as often as you eat this bread and drink the cup, you proclaim the Lord's death until he comes" (I Cor. 11:26). Paul wrote these words in response to an ecclesiastical disaster. The Lord's feast had become a calamity at Corinth precisely because the old divisions, such as that between rich and poor, had been allowed to continue or reappear within the Christian gatherings. Such schisms are sinful. When some treat the Lord's feast as if it were their own private banquet, it is no longer the Lord's feast, no matter how sacramental the intention. The rich who excommunicate the poor by eating all the food excommunicate themselves by their indifference to human need. Their selfishness is a betrayal of Jesus, sacrificing him on the altar of a religiosity that despises the humanity for which he died.

How Christians behave toward one another really matters. Not only do they proclaim the gospel in their meetings, but their meetings make the gospel known to the world. One way or another, their meals themselves proclaim what they are about. Just as Jesus' willingness to eat with sinners gave a message to the world, so the Corinthians' failure to eat and drink considerately together undoes whatever they say. The Lord's feast is itself a proclamation, for it enacts an understanding of life that honors the delicate and intricate relations between grace and gladness, gratitude and generosity.

Eating and drinking together in recognition of Jesus *celebrates* God as God. God is the giver of all good things, the founder of every feast, the true host of every meal. All humans are guests in God's world; and, as well-mannered guests should and do, they honor their host. At its heart, Christian worship is etiquette. It is a matter of manners, of expressing gratitude to the host of life and graciousness to the other guests. To eat or drink without regard for God is to deny the honor due the host; and to eat or drink without concern for the other guests is to deny the host's right to choose the guests. Every meal, therefore, is an occasion for worship, for eucharistic and ethical behavior; and every meal, as a gift from God, like those of the earliest disciples, for whom grace came "as they were eating," shares something of those crucial feasts where God's consummate gift is celebrated.

Chapter
V

THE LORD'S SERVICE

"Each of you contributes"

He . . . lufid vs in his goednes, noght for oure seruys.
—Richard Rolle,
Psalter xvii.22

Obliti privatorum publica curate.
—Rector's Palace,
Dubrovnik

'Tis mad idolatry
To make the service greater than the god.
—Shakespeare,
Troilus and Cressida

Greet one another with a holy kiss.
—I Corinthians 16:20

To sum up, my friends: when you meet for worship,
each of you contributes a hymn, some instruction,
a revelation, an ecstatic utterance, or the interpretation of such an utterance. All of these must aim
at one thing: to build up the church.
—I Corinthians 14:26, NEB

"Each of you contributes"

When Christians are gathered to celebrate reality as given and graced in Jesus, their assemblies, with or without feast, are often called "services." What they do together, depending upon the people involved, or the time, purposes, and place, may be designated as a eucharistic service, an evangelistic service, a prayer service, a Scripture service, the divine service, the morning service, the evening service, the service of worship, the worship service, or some other such permutation of words and meanings. Indeed, even if the people prefer the statelier term "liturgy" (which, after all, is simply "service" with Greek ancestry!), such occasions—no matter how various in character and composition, whether traditional or innovative, stylized or spontaneous, labyrinthine or simple, solemn or casual, staid or jaunty, with a vast throng or among a small coterie—are services.

I. But what does "service" mean? Latin in etymology, the word has accumulated an abundance of English usages and meanings. According to the *Oxford English Dictionary*, it primarily describes the condition or work of a servant, the fact or act of serving a master. From this basic meaning, it derives its several "religious" usages. It means "serving God" (whether through obedience, piety, or good works),

worship, a celebration of public worship, a ritual or series of
words and ceremonies prescribed for public worship, and a
musical setting, or a book, for use in services of worship. All
of these meanings, it may be observed, intimate that service
is something which humans do for God; and, by implication
at least, they tend to set worship within the context of the
servant-master image of relationship and reality. In fact,
from the very history of the language, it appears that at the
center of every *act* of service there lies the *state* (or condition) of servitude. Hence, to serve is to be engaged in, and
to enact, the relationship of servant to master. By such
lights, a service of worship is a more or less deliberate enactment of subservience. So understood, worship itself expresses, indeed celebrates, human dependence upon God.
Such, therefore, may be the meaning in the Septuagint,
where words for "serve," words like *douleuō*, *latreuō*, and
leitourgeō, are used to describe obligations owed, by priests
and people, directly to God as Lord.

In the New Testament, however, things appear to be
somehow different. There it is believed that the human
situation before God has been transformed in Jesus the
Christ. "No longer do I call you servants, for the servant
does not know what his master is doing; but I have called
you friends" (John 15:15). From within this perspective,
cultic activities and relationships, as well as the traditional
understandings of "serving God," seem questionable. In the
New Testament itself, it should be noted, *latreia* is resit-
uated in an ethical context (Rom. 12:1);[41] while *leitourgia*
is employed to speak of the "service" which Epaphroditus
gives to Paul (Phil. 2:30), or of the service rendered by the
offering sent to the congregation in Jerusalem (II Cor. 9:12).
Parenthetically, perhaps it deserves to be pondered that the
linguistic roots of our word "liturgy" extended so widely and

flourished so abundantly in the ancient world, yet they appear with what may seem such strange infrequency in the New Testament. Remarkably, what the New Testament does appear to seize upon is the ordinary, commonplace, and "secular" word for service, *diakoneō*. Absent from the Septuagint, it has its linguistic "home" in the everyday activity of waiting on tables. Thus, unlike *douleuō*, it denotes more an *act* of service, done on occasion, than a *state* of continuous servitude. So understood, serving may be an activity of free human beings, who freely choose to serve. This kind of serving, diaconal in character, while it may seem menial (Luke 22:27), embodies genuine helpfulness (Philemon 13), may be used to describe what prophets do (I Peter 1:12), is a worthy expression of love for God (Heb. 6:10), and is understood to be an apt summary of the ministry of Jesus (Matt. 20:28). Such serving is true ministry; and true ministry is such serving.

To speak of the "Lord's service," however, suggests an ambiguity—an ambiguity equally present in the German *Gottesdienst*, commonly translated "worship," but literally meaning "service of God." Is the genitive here objective or subjective? Is worship understood properly as the human service of God or as God's service of humans? Or is worship somehow both together, meeting in paradox, like the paradox of grace and freedom? Thus, obviously, the ambiguity is substantial, for it embraces the question of who does the worshiping as well as the question of who is served by the worshiping. On the question of who does the worshiping, the New Testament and much of the Christian tradition have affirmed that our worship is a consequence of God's working. Our worship is a response, a response in which we give thanks for all that God has done, is doing, and promises to do. Nevertheless, and beyond this, even our gratitude is to be understood as among the gracious workings of God among God's people. Thus, when it has known itself truly and well, the Christian tradition has been graced with a glad and emphatic recognition of the workings of the Spirit among the people. The apostle Paul, for example, in speaking of prayer, suggests that "through our inarticulate groans the Spirit himself is pleading for us" (Rom. 8:26, NEB). Or throughout The Acts of the Apostles, from the Day of Pentecost onward, whatever is done for good is done by the power of the Spirit. "And when they had prayed, the place in which they were gathered together was shaken; and they were all filled with the Holy Spirit and spoke the word of God with boldness" (Acts 4:31). Hence, in all their gatherings, one of the sure signs of the Spirit among them is their ecstatically joyful gladness *(agalliasis),* which simply overflows in praise (Acts 2:46–47). And definitively for the apostle Paul, especially in his extended discussion (I Corinthians 12–14) of the relations between the Spirit, the various gifts of the Spirit, and the community of love, God as Spirit is so indisputably active in worship that "no one can say 'Jesus is Lord!' except under the influence of the Holy Spirit" (I Cor. 12:3, NEB). For Paul and others, God is so active in all that we do that even our worship of God is ultimately a matter of God's own working among us. For us, of course, the relations between grace and freedom (as the tortured history of Christian understandings and misunderstandings more than amply reveals!) are subtly woven and textured. The question of who does the worshiping is not now easily unraveled. Therefore, in what may be a felicitous ambiguity, worship is the "service of God."

But who receives this service? Is worship (whether it be God's activity or ours, or somehow both together) service for God or for humans? In a way, of course, this issue was touched upon earlier (in the discussion of "Why Worship?"); but there the real emphasis was upon the theological truism that, as humans, women and men must celebrate or die. For genuine humans, grace and gratitude inherently belong together—like inhaling and exhaling!

Is worship for God or for humans? Whom is it supposed to benefit? That the question has ordinarily been posed this way may express an understanding of reality unaffected by grace. In many conceptions of reality (whether ancient or modern), it should be remembered, *power* is conceived of as being the central concept. Who, or what, has power? Where did it come from? How can power be gained? Or increased? How can it be protected? How can it be lost? Such are some of the classic issues flowing from the question of power; and, often underlying them, there are the assumptions (frequently unquestioned) that power is not only the truly dominant reality but that power itself implies, indeed requires, dominion over something or someone. Theologically, such notions often set gods and humans against one another. They are imagined as competitors for power, struggling for the strength to be or to become themselves. They are thought to be rivals. Thus Prometheus, who steals fire from heaven and gives it to earth, is punished by Zeus. And similarly, perhaps, the serpent tempts Eve, promising her that eating the fruit will make her "like God, knowing good and evil" (Gen. 3:5). Wherever reality is understood hierarchically, insubordination is the primal sin—whether the insubordination be familial, political, or theological. The master image is that of lord and servants. As between John the Baptist and Jesus, so between humans and God, "He must increase, but I must decrease." Not surprisingly there is, it seems, a kind of seesaw or teeter-totter principle acting pivotally in many theories of worship. By such lights, hu-

mans are thought to be slaves of God; as slaves they are
made to serve God; and their worship, basically, is their
slavish subservience. Therefore, within many traditional
world views, where God is conceived of primarily in terms
of power, and where power is understood to be a threat to
power, being properly captive to deity requires of humans an
attitude of powerlessness. Within such hierarchical world
views, where even upholding human dignity might be inter-
preted as a dishonoring of the divine stature, worship is
normally defined as homage, requiring obeisance and prostration before God.

II.   Throughout the ancient world, gestures of defer-
ence were everyday occurrences, as "inferiors" showed due
respect for "superiors." Bowing, kneeling, throwing a kiss,
kissing someone's feet or the hem of someone's garment,
biting the dust, or prostration were acknowledgments of the
power of the other over one. Thus, for example, when the
Lord appeared by the oaks of Mamre, Abraham "bowed low
to the ground" (Gen. 18:2, NEB). Or when a fearful Jacob
is confronted by Esau and four hundred men, Jacob timor-
ously greets his brother by "bowing low to the ground seven
times" (Gen. 33:3, NEB). Such "bowing *down*," which may
be translated as "worship," expresses an attitude, both physi-
cally and mentally. It is an act of submission. Hence, Psalm
99:5 says:

> Exalt the LORD our God,
>   bow down before his footstool;
>   he is holy.
>   (NEB)

Or, in a more customary, but less literal translation:

> Extol the LORD our God;
>   worship at his footstool!
>   Holy is he!
>   (RSV)

For much of the Old Testament, whether in Hebrew or in the Greek of the Septuagint, "bowing down" and "worship" are linguistic equivalents. Thus, according to George E. Mendenhall:

> The symbolic action denoted by the Old Testament Hebrew term consists of kneeling before the god or person having power, and then leaning forward until the face rests on the ground, or sometimes becoming completely prostrate. Sometimes the act is completed and acknowledged by the god's or king's placing his foot on the head or neck of the worshiper. The symbolisms should not be difficult to understand. The situation is that typified by a captive of war. The man has been rendered powerless by superior power, and henceforth his fate is completely in the hands of the mighty one. He is in a state of absolute dependence upon the will of the victor, and this is the first basic significance of the act.[42]

From such a perspective, incidentally, it is worth noting that the Islamic term "mosque" derives from an Arabic word *masjid,* meaning "place of prostration."[43]

In the Septuagint, the term that embraces the meanings of "worship" and "bowing down" is *proskyneō.* The word itself is very interesting. Its root is *kyneō* ("kiss"), which, curiously, gives it a basis analogous to that of the Latin *os,* as in "osculate," or *ora,* as in "oral," "orate," and "adoration."[44] The Vulgate, therefore, translates *proskyneō* as *adoro.* Perhaps humans are so ineluctably embodied that even their gestures leave verbal vestiges of their import; or

the gestures simply outlive their rationales! Thus, according
to Homer, when Odysseus returned safely to land, "he
kissed the earth, the giver of grain" (*Odyssey* 13:354). Just
like an astronaut?

In the New Testament, the verb *proskyneō* appears about
sixty times. More than twenty of these occurrences are in
the book of Revelation; and the word is most frequently translated as "worship." However, although the word does occur
with noticeable frequency, its usage deserves some scrutiny.
The Wise Men seek to "worship" (Matt. 2:2). The tempter
seeks "worship" (Matt. 4:9). A ruler, seeking help, "knelt
before" Jesus (Matt. 9:18). In a parable, the verb is used of
a servant before a king (Matt. 18:26), and of the soldiers who
mocked Jesus (Mark 15:19). Those who "worship" God
must "worship" in spirit and truth (John 4:24). In a speech
in Acts, Paul says he went up to "worship" at Jerusalem
(Acts 24:11). And at Corinth an outsider might "worship"
(I Cor. 14:23–25):

> If, therefore, the whole church assembles and all speak in
> tongues, and outsiders or unbelievers enter, will they not say
> that you are mad? But if all prophesy, and an unbeliever or
> outsider enters, he is convicted by all, he is called to account
> by all, the secrets of his heart are disclosed; and so, falling on
> his face, he will worship God and declare that God is really
> among you.

This reference, the only usage of the term in the Pauline
letters, is particularly illuminating, precisely because it is not
here a Christian, but an *outsider*, who so "worships" God.
As Bo Reicke observes, "Nowhere in the New Testament
does *proskyneō* mean technical worship performed by Christians on this earth."[45] From one perspective, obviously,
since *proskyneō* involves some directionality, those who may

have prostrated themselves at Jesus' feet now have no place
toward which to turn. From another perspective, they, like
the outsider, may turn to the community. But, it appears,
only an outsider will do even that. Perhaps, finally, the force
of the evidence suggests that in the New Testament, and
among the Christians at least, what may well have been,
previously, the very pivotal gesture and notion of worship in
the religions of homage and obeisance has now been over-
thrown. The gods had been thought to dwell on sacred
mountains, in temples or shrines, or in various theopolitical
personages. The ancient gods deserved due respect; indeed,
they were imaged as living by it and thriving on it. They
deserved, required, and received *proskynēsis*. However,
something new is being revealed in the New Testament. A
profound shift in world view is making itself felt; and perhaps at the very heart of the shift is the amazing notion of
God as giver.

Israel, of course, had known the notion. Indeed, it may
be seen as the gracious center of the covenant between
Yahweh and Israel; but within the New Testament itself
there is an obvious move from notions of God as conquering
hero to an understanding of God as generous host. The
consequences are enormous, as enormous as the differences,
even the chasm, between power and love. In much of the
ancient world, human worth was estimated in terms of the
number of slaves one had power over. The more slaves, the
more worth; the more at one's disposal, the more exalted one
was. Since power is power in relation, the powerful proved
their power by rendering their rivals powerless. Masters
thrive on slavery. They are captives to it. If, however, the
image shifts, and the model is no longer master/servants but
host/guests, there is a world of difference. Hosts, genuinely
gracious hosts, are not competitors of their guests. Indeed,

a good host is measured by the criteria of love, not power. What matters is the guests' delight. This new image is clear in Luke:

> A dispute arose also between them about which should be reckoned the greatest, but he said to them, "Among pagans it is the kings who lord it over them, and those who have authority over them are given the title Benefactor. This must not happen with you. No; the greatest among you must behave as if he were the youngest, the leader as if he were the one who serves. For who is the greater: the one at table or the one who serves? The one at table, surely? Yet here am I among you as one who serves!" (Luke 22:24–27, JB)

Here the image of reality is being redrawn. The love of power is being transformed by the power of love; and Jesus' disciples are being beckoned into helpfulness. Those who would picture Christians as soldiers, captured and conscripted into some heavenly army, slavishly taking orders and dutifully saluting, have it all wrong; for among the testimonies of the New Testament, another design is being sketched. Imagine a lavish feast, generously thrown by a host whose love and provisions seem to know no bounds. All sorts of guests have been invited, without any lines or limits; and, at the feast, the host's own child sets the style for all by waiting on tables. At such a feast, wonderfully, all are guests and all are waiters. Each gives worth and delight to all the others, as the host's graciousness animates the glad occasion.

In the New Testament, as Christians gather, their characteristic gesture is not *proskynēsis*. God, it is believed, does not require or desire human abasement. *Proskynēsis* is abandoned by Christians because God does not seek it, no human deserves it, and no thing is worthy of it. Instead, the

Christians' "salute," so to speak, is a greeting shared among themselves. In words that resonate like a liturgical formula, Paul enjoins the members of the congregations: "Greet one another with a holy kiss" (Rom. 16:16; I Cor. 16:20; II Cor. 13:12).[46] The salute of "inferiors" to "superiors" has been replaced by the gesture of friendship. Among Christians, *proskynēsis* is replaced by *philēma,* abasement is surpassed by companionship! In their greetings of one another, they share the worth each has received. Thus, in his treatise on prayer, Tertullian speaks of this kiss, the "kiss of peace" *(osculum pacis),* as the "sealing of prayer" *(signaculum orationis)* and asks, "What prayer is complete without the bond of a holy kiss?"[47] For him, as for the apostle Paul, the integrity of prayer and the integrity of community are interdependent. A true honoring of God gives humans stature; it gets them off their knees and to their feet. It builds them, up and together.

Writing in a time when Christians customarily met in someone's "home" *(oikos),* Paul aptly uses the metaphor of building, edifying, upbuilding *(oikodomeō).* In a religious world, filled with temples and shrines, Paul tells the Christians at Corinth that *they* are "God's building" *(oikodomē;* I Cor. 3:9). Paul's apostolic authority, unlike the authority of those who subdue kingdoms and put down peoples, is "to build you up, not pull you down" (II Cor. 10:8, NEB). And he reminds the Christians, troubled over such questions as appropriate food and drink, to "pursue the things that make for peace and build up the common life" (Rom. 14:19, NEB). The whole purpose of "ministry" *(diakonia)* is "for building up the body of Christ" (Eph. 4:12), a body which, when functioning properly, "upbuilds itself in love" (Eph. 4:16). As Hugh M. Scott summarizes:

Apostolic worship meant, accordingly, an immediate appro-
priation of the good things of God in Christ. It was no longer
pursuit; it was possession; hence the leading thought in this
early devotion was not so much worshiping God as it was
edifying the brethren. Not even praising Christ was the chief
duty, but rather building up His body, the Church in love.[48]

Or as Erasmus wrote at the beginning of the sixteenth
century:

And do not tell me, presently, that charity consists of fre-
quent church attendance or genuflecting in front of the images of saints or burning candles or repeating a specified
number of little prayers. God is not impressed by such rou-
tines. Paul calls it love to raise up one's neighbor, to consider
all men as members of the same Body. . . . So we should be
devoted to the welfare of others, not to our own.[49]

In the New Testament, for the apostle Paul at least, the
fundamental criterion, as Christians gather for worship, is
neither service to God, nor service to the self, nor even
perhaps service to the neighbor, but the nourishment,
growth, and graced delight of the community. "The language of ecstasy is good for the speaker himself, but it is
prophecy that builds up a Christian community" (I Cor.
14:4, NEB). In truly Christian worship, the Spirit works
among the gathered people as each person ministers to the
upbuilding of the whole.

III.   The Lord's service, understood as God working
through persons to create a genuinely human community,
suffuses and permeates all of life. Such, obviously, is the
import of Paul's appeal: "Therefore, my brothers, I implore

you by God's mercy to offer your very selves to him: a living sacrifice, dedicated and fit for his acceptance, the worship offered by mind and heart" (Rom. 12:1, NEB). Therefore, no occasion or dimension of life is truly lived apart from worship. Life itself is helping build. Consequently, whatever Christians do when they gather for worship is to be done in the grateful recognition that all life has already been hallowed by grace.

Nevertheless, and from within such an understanding, gathered Christians do have "services of worship," in which they are engaged by the Spirit and they share their gratitude, their gladness, and their gifts. Since the early Christians, there have been assemblies on the Lord's Day to share the Lord's feast. Whatever else was or was not done, whether elaborately or simply, "breaking bread in their homes, they partook of food with glad and generous hearts" (Acts 2:46). Yet beyond such profound simplicities, the evidence tends to blur, to be sketchy and indefinite. According to Acts 2:42, "They devoted themselves to the apostles' teaching and to the fellowship, to the breaking of bread and to prayer" (NIV). Some scholars read this as a report of an early "order of worship" (with sermon, offering, meal, and prayers), but their arguments, while attractive to many, are inconclusive.[50] Given the idealized character of the community depicted in the early chapters of Acts, we simply cannot be sure precisely what occurred, or in what order, in the earliest assemblies.

In Paul's letters, however, there are numerous clues, indicating what may have transpired in the early Christian gatherings.

Let the word of Christ dwell in you richly, teach and admonish one another in all wisdom, and sing psalms and hymns

> and spiritual songs with thankfulness in your hearts to God.
> And whatever you do, in word or deed, do everything in the
> name of the Lord Jesus, giving thanks to God the Father
> through him. (Col. 3:16–17)

> And do not get drunk with wine, for that is debauchery; but
> be filled with the Spirit, addressing one another in psalms and
> hymns and spiritual songs, singing and making melody to the
> Lord with all your heart, always and for everything giving
> thanks in the name of our Lord Jesus Christ to God the
> Father. (Eph. 5:18–20)

In the context of thanksgivings, perhaps after the meal as
in the Jewish custom, there were teachings and songs! Some
of the songs, incidentally, may be found in Luke 1:46–55,
68–79; 2:29–32; Eph. 5:14; Phil. 2:5–11; I Tim. 3:16; and
throughout Revelation.[51] Perhaps another listing of components to the "service" appears in Romans 12, where worship
is understood as the exercise of "gifts":

> Having gifts that differ according to the grace given to us, let
> us use them: if prophecy, in proportion to our faith; if service,
> in our serving; he who teaches, in his teaching; he who
> exhorts, in his exhortation; he who contributes, in liberality;
> he who gives aid, with zeal; he who does acts of mercy, with
> cheerfulness. (Rom. 12:6–8)

The most helpful evidence, however, concerning the early
Christian gatherings may be found in I Corinthians 12–14,
which provides "a richer insight into community life than
any other passage in the New Testament."[52] In what may
describe the festivities following the feast (Is this the rationale behind Eph. 5:18, for the placement of I Cor. 12 after
the discussion of the feast in I Cor. 11, as well as for the
mention of the "thanksgiving" in I Cor. 14:16?), Paul refers
to many activities, activities as multifarious as the persons

involved, to whom they are given as gifts: the utterance of wisdom, the utterance of knowledge, faith, gifts of healing, the working of miracles, prophecy, discernment, "tongues," and the interpretation of "tongues" (I Cor. 12:7–11). Or, according to I Corinthians 14, the assembled Christians prophesy, speak in tongues, understand, utter mysteries, interpret, bring revelation, knowledge, prophecy, or teaching, know, pray, sing, bless, say "Amen," give thanks, instruct, keep silence, weigh, and learn.

> To sum up, my friends: when you meet for worship, each of you contributes a hymn, some instruction, a revelation, an ecstatic utterance, or the interpretation of such an utterance.
> (I Cor. 14:26, NEB)

Clearly, here at least, there is no fixed order; but, lest there be confusion from everything happening at once, "everything should be done in a fitting and orderly way" (I Cor. 14:40, NIV). In other words, people are to take turns! What really matters, however, is not so much precisely what is done, or in what sequence. The lists differ. Plainly, what does matter, and matters profoundly, is that everyone makes use of whatever gifts each has received. Precisely because worship is "upbuilding" not abasement, and because what each has received is a "gift" from God, Christian assemblies truly honor God as each individual contributes to all. The gifts may vary in significance. Surely to speak a clear and helpful word of reality surpasses ecstatic speech! Nevertheless, to neglect or stifle anyone's "gift" *(charisma)*, no matter how strange, may, ultimately, be a refusal of "grace" *(charis)*, cheating the community of what God wants it to have. Thus, in ways beyond what even Paul may have imagined, truly Christian assemblies are gatherings of women, men, and children, where those with gifts for singing and speaking, hearing and helping, praying and pondering, discussing and discerning, counseling and caring, encouraging and empowering, exercise their gifts for one another. Faithfulness requires sharing! In the memorable words of Isaac Watts:

> Let those refuse to sing
>   Who never knew our God;
> But children of the heavenly King
>   May speak their joys abroad.

Everyone is to do something! Of course, there may well be a sermon; but monotonous and monolithic worship, where the focus is upon one person, who throws sermons like stones into a lake of listeners, trusting the ripples to reach to all, is questionable. Instead, in genuinely Christian worship, all are somehow together engaged (to borrow the exquisite phrase of Nelle Morton) in the act of "hearing each other into speech";[53] and everyone, even the least gifted or the most reticent, is truly expected to sing, to share, to pray, to help, to "understand," to "weigh" what is said and done, and to say the "Amen"![54]

IV.   As Christians are gathered to *celebrate* the Lord who has become a servant, joining and hosting the feast of life, they rejoice together in the gifts that each has received. Somewhat like glad children at Christmas, they show their delight by playing with their gifts; but, in what may measure their growth, they find joy in discovering what others also have been given. Truly to celebrate is to be glad in the joys of others.

Those who participate in the Lord's service *acknowledge* God as the giver of gifts. They recognize God as gracious.

Their worship is conceived in grace and born in thanksgiving, thanksgiving to the God whose favor and generosity are unmeasured. Those who assemble, assemble in the recognition that God's gifts are diverse. Therefore, no one person, alone, now speaks for God. The manifold graciousness of God requires diversity for its true acknowledgment. Therefore, as the New Testament knows so well, God's grace manifests itself in a genuinely healthy pluralism. Thus, even though the gifts may vary in worth (so that "prophecy" is more helpful than "tongues"), none is to be despised, and all are to be received with thanksgiving. Consequently, no one person's piety is to be made normative; and no one principle or person is to be fixed over all the others. Note, incidentally, that the closest Paul, for example, ever came to such fixing was in I Corinthians 13, where he suggested "love"; but love itself is neither a principle nor a person. Love is a relationship. And, by the way, even Paul is only one apostle among several! In the Lord's service, diversity of gifts is to be acknowledged and honored. Furthermore, there is a recognition that the benefits of God's gifts, indeed the gifts themselves, come to us through others; and the fullness of grace, for anyone, comes through the interdependence of the gifted. No one can go it alone. Not only do all need grace, but they need it from each other. Each alone, without all, is less than truly human. Therefore, for the sake of all, all are ministers, called to serve. "Whatever gift each of you may have received, use it in service to one another, like good stewards dispensing the grace of God in its varied forms" (I Peter 4:10, NEB).

Those who participate in the Lord's service *rehearse* life as it is meant to be. In their assemblies, in which they acknowledge human interdependence, with its many virtues and vulnerabilities, its strengths and its risks, they struggle

to model and empower life understood as service. In a world
where the "strong" do not admit their need of the "weak,"
in a world where the "rich" do not sense their need of the
"poor," and where "adults" do not know the need for "children," or in a world where the interdependence of "men"
and "women" is denied or distorted, Christian assemblies
are called together to rehearse patterns and styles of mutual
recognition and empowerment. The measure of their mutuality, of their service to one another, is a harbinger of a world
hallowed by grace. Their assemblies are to experiment, ex-
ploring the scope and directions of the divine purposes for
the world, thereby becoming enabled, willing, and ready
agents for the subversion of everything that threatens the
real dignity and full stature of any human being.

Therefore, when Christian assemblies truly celebrate the
Lord's service, those who participate, together and severally,
proclaim what God has done, is doing, and promises to do
in the world. Their message forms their life; and their life
itself is a proclamation. Everything they do should be appropriate testimony to the Lord who serves. Even their openness to the despised, the rejected, the insecure, the hesitant,
the doubters, and the simply curious, is a sure test of their
authenticity. Truly to serve, their assemblies should be such
as to prompt outsiders to confess that "God is really among
you" (I Cor. 14:25). Indeed, the very purpose of their being
together may well be to affirm and exemplify the winsome-
ness of God's grace.

As their gatherings are built up in the Lord's service, every
member grows and the whole company grows. Each member is to grow up, to mature in using the gifts all have been
given; and new members are welcomed, both as those with
whom grace is to be shared and as those whose presence
swells the diversity of gifts available for all. The rationale for

evangelism is simple. The assembly proclaims the reality it has received; and the community is given new members who add their testimony to the proclamation of the depths and diversity of grace. The purpose is clear: "But you are a chosen race, a royal priesthood, a dedicated nation, and a people claimed by God for his own, to proclaim the triumphs of him who has called you out of darkness into his marvellous light" (I Peter 2:9, NEB). In the Lord's service, "each of you contributes"!

Chapter
VI

THE LORD'S WELCOME

"The Lord added to their group"

Consider the journey from Shittim to Gilgal,
in order that you may know the triumph
   of the LORD.
                              —Micah 6:5, NEB

Let us, then, draw from the river as much help as
we require.
                              —Origen,
                                 Commentary on John

And every day the Lord added to their group those
who were being saved.
                              —Acts 2:47, TEV

For all of you who were baptized into Christ have
been clothed with Christ. There is neither Jew nor
Greek, slave nor free, male nor female, for you are
all one in Christ Jesus.
                              —Galatians 3:27–28, NIV

Prepared for the supper of the Lamb,
Radiant in our white robes,
Having passed through the Red Sea,
Let us sing to Christ the Lord.
                              —*Ad cenam agni providi*

Welcome to the ministry of Jesus Christ.
                              —*The Worshipbook* (1972),
                                 The Sacrament of
                                 Baptism

"The Lord added to their group"

Acts and words belong together, clarifying and reinforcing each other. Sometimes word defines action; sometimes action confirms word. Often words demand actions. "Don't speak of love. Show me!" Or, frequently, actions deserve words. "You act as if you love me, but please tell me that you do. Please, say it!" Thus, when humans meet, the words and gestures of greeting belong together. There is a suitable symmetry between gesture and word. We somehow recognize that a simple "Hello!" and a fond embrace are mismatched. They don't suit each other. They are as incongruous as vowing "I love you!" while only shaking hands. The true relations between words and actions are intricate and intimate. They need each other. Indeed, actions and words may empower and sustain each other against emptiness—since, apart and alone, words or gestures are always in danger of becoming vacuous formalities. Words without actions may become "mere talk," the chatter of sociable parrots. Deeds are often needed to embody words, implementing them in reality. Deeds, however, often need the defining explanations which only words can give. Wordless deeds, "empty rituals," as Calvin knew and others have known so well, can easily become as meaningless as the mimicry of monkeys. Indeed, in a word, neither monkeys nor parrots are the epitome of human communication. Nevertheless, some genuinely human actions may sometimes communicate wordlessly. Their meaning is defined, silently, by unspoken behavioral patterns, cultural traditions, and social contexts. Thus, whenever relationships are sure and meanings are actually shared, actions may be given, may have, and may even appear to possess intrinsically, communicative power.

If this is true, then it should no longer surprise us that the New Testament seems to offer so little help in answering our fundamental questions about baptism. After all, what "everybody knows" is seldom written down; and, when everybody knew what "baptizing" was and meant, there was no obvious reason to describe or discuss it. In our culture, similarly perhaps, where everybody understands "shaking hands," no one takes time and bother to help some future generation comprehend precisely what is implied by those very ordinary and yet curiously ambiguous words. Even in the otherwise precise stage directions for plays, this action is simply indicated but not explained. Yet, quite remarkably, when you think about it, the phrase is not itself responsive and forthcoming to even so simple yet significant a question as whether the "shaking hands" ever touch! Was baptism by immersion? Did the baptizer touch the baptizand? What clothes were worn, if any? Who was usually present? Did anybody say anything? If so, who and what? And, as we pose such really unremarkable questions, seeking to grasp hold of some firm answers, what actually happened seems to float, as it were, tantalizingly just beyond our reach. Perhaps everybody knew so much and understood it so well that nobody was moved to write much of anything about it.

What the New Testament itself does seem to report is that many "baptisms" took place; and that "baptizing," like "drowning" (which may be the original meaning of the word), is an *action with water*. It is worth notice that the verb "baptize" *(baptizō)* occurs more than seventy times in the New Testament, while the noun "baptism" *(baptisma)* occurs only about twenty times. According to all four Gospels, directly or by implication, the ministry of Jesus as the Christ was inaugurated at the time of his baptism by John the Baptist in the Jordan. In the New Testament, this baptism of Jesus may be the fundamental rationale for the baptizing of those who are becoming Christians. In any event, the apostle Paul, whose references to baptism are crucial, appears to offer no rationale for baptism itself. For him, it seems, baptism is a given; and he argues from its actuality, as universal among Christians, to its ethical implications. His logic runs: Since you have been baptized, therefore behave! Perhaps the only actual definition of baptism in the New Testament is found in I Peter: Baptism "now saves you also—not [as] the removal of dirt from the body but [as] the pledge of a good conscience toward God. It saves you by the resurrection of Jesus Christ" (I Peter 3:21, NIV). Such, in sum, may be the basic New Testament testimony concerning baptism.[55]

I. Water, of course, in many cultures, has profound reservoirs of meaning. It would be strange if it were otherwise. Water, after all, enlivens humans. Simply at the biological level, it is the "only substance necessary to all life; many organisms can live without oxygen, but none can live without water."[56] Consequently, at or near the surface of consciousness, especially for those who have lived in deserts or in the lands of the Bible, is the recognition that without the "waters of life" everything living dries up and blows away! Water is a basic agent of vitality. All of us were born from it; and, throughout our lives, we somehow must satisfy our thirst or die. No wonder Thales thought it to be the primal substance; or that, in Greek mythology, Oceanus and Tethys were named the parents of the gods; or that, according to the ancient cosmogony of Mesopotamia (literally, "between the rivers"), everything came from the primeval waters of Apsu and Tiamat. In Egypt, water was male (promising fertility); in Babylonia, water was female (promising fecundity). Throughout the ancient world, life was surrounded and determined by water. There were rivers of life, rivers of death, and fountains of youth. Water was chaotic and creative, bringing both terror and refreshment; and, in the arid places, water was the heart and promise of every oasis. Even in the modern world, where technology may disguise and distort the full measure of our dependence upon cosmic resources, water still fascinates humans. We will travel miles upon miles to get near it or into it. Lakes appear to promise serenity; water occasions recreation; and even toddlers traipse through puddles with glee. In the Roman Empire, the baths were gathering places, offering public space for human encounters; while for some in our time, swimming pools may serve similar social functions. Furthermore, in several cultures, those who have been ill almost invariably take a bath and put on fresh clothes to signal their recovery. Surely, for them, water marks the boundary between sickness and health. And, throughout the world, water describes many, if not most, of the major geographic and political boundaries. In fact, water is so significant to so many dimensions of human reality that a modern poet sings its praises in his poem "Water," which begins:

> If I were called in
> To construct a religion
> I should make use of water.[57]

Throughout the Bible, water is given a momentous role both in creation and in redemption. In the Priestly saga of cosmic creation (Gen. 1:1 to 2:4a), the earth itself emerges out of a watery chaos. Water is, so to speak, the womb from which life springs; water is the fountain, the source of all earthly realities. Thus, the prophets speak of God as "the fountain of living waters" (Jer. 2:13), promising to "pour water on the thirsty land" (Isa. 44:3). The psalmist affirms:

> The earth is the LORD's and all that is in it,
>   the world and those who dwell therein.
> For it was he who founded it upon the seas
>   and planted it firm upon the waters beneath.
>   (Ps. 24:1–2, NEB)

The New Testament mirrors this aqueous imagery as it tells of "an earth formed out of water and by means of water" (II Peter 3:5); and there may be an allusion to these cosmic waters, as well as to the waters of baptism, as Paul speaks of the "new creation" (*kainē ktisis*), proclaiming, "When anyone is united to Christ, there is a new world" (II Cor. 5:17, NEB). Nevertheless, if water creates, it also threatens. If it is womb, it is also tomb. Thus, in the story of Noah and the Flood (Gen. 6:5 to 8:22), waters act as agents of judgment. Waters drown the wicked. The only hope is an ark that gives safe passage through the waters. According to the New Testament, the world "was deluged with water and perished" (II Peter 3:6), while Noah and his family, the eight persons, "were saved through water" (I Peter 3:20). Hence, though the waters may afford passage to safety, they retain their powers for judgment and terror, so the seer dreams of an ultimate realm where and when "the sea was no more" (Rev. 21:1), though even in that realm there is "the river of the water of life, bright as crystal, flowing from the throne of God and of the Lamb" (Rev. 22:1).

Israel's central story, however, shaping and reshaping the watery sagas of creation and redemption, is the event of the rescue at the Red Sea (Ex. 13:17 to 14:31). Water is the solvent, separating and liberating Israel from Egypt while routing and drowning the Egyptians. In the words of the psalmist:

> Thy way was through the sea,
>   thy path through the great waters;
>   yet thy footprints were unseen.
> Thou didst lead thy people like a flock
>   by the hand of Moses and Aaron.
>   (Ps. 77:19–20)

In the formative traditions of Israel, this was *the* redemptive event, an event without equal. There were parallels, to be sure, but in the traditions it seems to have surpassed and transformed them all. In Second Isaiah, for example, the Lord's triumph at the Red Sea has a grandeur that evokes images of the primal creative combat with chaos. For the prophet, the Egyptians and the sea monsters of the ancient cosmogonies are conflated (Isa. 51:9–10). Redemption and creation are as one. Deliverance is a rescue from the depths; it is the passage through the waters. Hence, recalling this definitive event, the apostle Paul writes that "our fathers were all under the cloud, and all passed through the sea, and all were baptized into Moses in the cloud and in the sea" (I Cor. 10:1–2). Or, as expressed in the classic song of Miriam:

> I will sing to the LORD, for he has risen up in triumph;
> the horse and his rider he has hurled into the sea.
>   (Ex. 15:21, NEB)

Perhaps in recollection of this song and its image of rising up in triumph from the waters, the New Testament authors speak of Jesus as "raised" from the dead; Mark reports that Jesus "came up out of the water" at his baptism (Mark 1:10); and Paul relates baptism to the death and resurrection of Jesus: "We were buried therefore with him by baptism into death, so that as Christ was raised from the dead by the glory of the Father, we too might walk in newness of life" (Rom. 6:4).

Throughout the Bible, perhaps by analogy from the waters of the exodus, there is the theme of water as cleansing. For many, cleanliness is godliness; and water washes well. Elisha tells Naaman, "Go and wash in the Jordan seven times, and your flesh shall be restored, and you shall be clean" (II Kings 5:10). In Isaiah the people are told, "Wash yourselves; make yourselves clean" (Isa. 1:16). And Leviticus specifies the various requirements and rituals for cleanliness. Because of sin, and the people's need for cleansing, there are promises of water (Zech. 13:1 and Ezek. 36:25). Such imagery, obviously, is behind the assurance of Heb. 10:22: "with our hearts sprinkled clean from an evil conscience and our bodies washed with pure water."

Consequently, as Aidan Kavanagh summarizes,

> Receiving the Spirit through Christ is likened to a *birth bath* in John 3.3–5 and Titus 3.5–7; to a *funeral bath* and burial in Romans 6.1–11; to a bride's *nuptial bath* in Ephesians 5.26. These cultural practices were consummated in anointing and in arraying the body in clean, new, or otherwise special clothing (Galatians 3.27) as the final stages of the bath itself.[58]

Obviously, the theme of bathing, washing, or cleansing is significant; and it appears to have dominated much of the thinking about baptism. Nevertheless, it may be worth pondering whether it should become the only theme, as well as whether the New Testament itself is all of one mind about such actions with water. According to Luke, for example, a Pharisee is astonished that Jesus does not observe the ritual prescription about washing before meals; and his concern occasions Jesus to speak about true cleanliness as giving (Luke 11:37–41). In I Peter 3:21, while baptism "saves," it saves "not as a removal of dirt from the body." Incidentally, some hesitation about seeing baptism primarily as cleansing may be intimated by the *Apostolic Tradition* of Hippolytus, where those who are to be baptized are instructed to wash and cleanse themselves, as part of getting ready, *before* their baptism. Even bathing, after all, may be but a prelude to that radical passing through the waters which the New Testament understands as baptism.

II.   The Jordan threads its way through Israel's history. In many respects, it is the decisive river of human history, affecting peoples far beyond the narrow, winding, and shallow reaches of its waters. "In the enigma of its influence, the Jordan is without compare."[59] Among those whose lives were directly touched by its waters are Joshua, Elijah and Elisha, John the Baptist and Jesus.

To get from Shittim to Gilgal, Joshua and the Israelites had to cross the Jordan (Josh. 3:1 to 5:12). The Jordan was the final boundary between the wilderness wanderings and the conquest of the Promised Land. Israel left Egypt across water; Israel enters the Promised Land across water. The parallels between the crossing of the Red Sea and the crossing of the Jordan are remarkable. In both events, Yahweh

separates the waters, creating a pathway for Israel; at both
the Red Sea and the Jordan, the crossing is processional; in
conjunction with each of these journeys through the waters,
people are circumcised and the Passover is celebrated; and
each event has a hero, whether Moses or Joshua. "On that
day the LORD exalted Joshua in the sight of all Israel; and
they stood in awe of him, as they had stood in awe of Moses,
all the days of his life" (Josh. 4:14). Incidentally, the parallels
between Moses and Joshua are numerous and significant.
See, for example, Ex. 3:5 and Josh. 5:15! And, it should be
underlined, waters (the Jordan near Jericho) were also separated for Elijah and Elisha (II Kings 2:1–14).

Nevertheless, for all these illustrious figures of Israel, Yahweh is the real hero. "For the LORD your God dried up the
waters of the Jordan for you until you passed over, as the
LORD your God did to the Red Sea, which he dried up for
us until we passed over" (Josh. 4:23). Hence, according to
the poetic imagination, in the presence of Yahweh and for
Israel, the two separated waters have become as one:

> What ails you, O sea, that you flee?
> O Jordan, that you turn back?
> (Ps. 114:5)

And, according to the prophet, the people are to recall the
Jordan:

> Consider the journey from Shittim to Gilgal,
> in order that you may know the triumph of the LORD.[60]
> (Micah 6:5, NEB)

They are commanded to "put away the gods which your
fathers served beyond the River, and in Egypt, and serve the
LORD" (Josh. 24:14). Perhaps, after Jordan, the fundamental
question is not of dirt but of Egypt, not pollution but refusal

of the promise; and the action indicated is not bathing but passage through the waters. The Jordan is the boundary; and it was at this *boundary* that John the Baptist centered his ministry.

> The Jordan was central in the life of John, as it was in the life of Jesus, whom he baptized in its waters, and in the life of Elijah with whom both of them were spiritually linked. To the Jordan all three of them repaired at important crises in their lives, seeking solace and inspiration by its banks and in the wastelands nearby.[61]

It was in the Jordan that Jesus was baptized. The Jordan! In the Gospels, the Jordan is mentioned fifteen times; and, with an exquisite concreteness, each of the four Gospels joins Jesus to John, Elijah, and the Jordan; and, in the popular mind, there was some confusion between Jesus, John the Baptist, and Elijah (Matt. 16:13–16). Jesus identifies John the Baptist as "Elijah" (Matt. 17:9–13); and, when Jesus is transfigured, Moses and Elijah appear with him (Matt. 17:1–8).

But what about Joshua? Where is any mention of him? In the New Testament, according to Karl Barth, there is a "surprising" silence concerning "the story of Israel's entry into the promised land."[62] Or is there? Surely there was little need to mention Joshua among the earliest Christians, who must have known that the very name "Jesus" is "Joshua"! Allowing for shifts in Hebrew, Aramaic, and Greek, the names are at one in meaning "Yahweh saves"! Furthermore, lest this be considered simply as linguistic coincidence, it may be remembered that Israel's forty years of wandering in the wilderness before the Jordan are matched by Jesus' forty days of temptations in the wilderness after the Jordan. Thus, since he followed John the

Baptist as Joshua followed Moses, Jesus' ministry is anchored in the Jordan. Surely, anyone familiar with the traditions of Israel could scarcely hear mention of the Jordan and Jesus together without also thinking of Joshua. Like Sherwood Forest and Robin Hood, Gettysburg and Lincoln, or the theory of relativity and Einstein, it went without saying that the Jordan and Joshua belonged together.

Thus, all four Gospels relate Jesus to the Jordan and seem to be written with parallels to Joshua in mind. In the Synoptic Gospels, not only does Jesus' public service begin with his baptism at the Jordan, but at a crucial turning point he undertakes a ministry in Judea "beyond the Jordan" (Mark 10:1; Matt. 19:1) before his final journey to Jerusalem. In the Gospel of John, the phrase "beyond the Jordan" occurs three times. In John 1:28, it specifies where John was baptizing. As Raymond E. Brown notes:

> John may be calling attention to the Joshua-Jesus parallelism. Just as Joshua led the people *across* the Jordan into the promised land, so Jesus is to *cross over* into the promised land at the head of a new people. Pilgrim tradition identifies the same site on the Jordan for both Joshua's crossing and Jesus' baptism.[63]

In John 3:26, people speak of Jesus as the one who was with John "beyond the Jordan," and is now himself baptizing. For John, however, Jesus' definitive "sign" is the raising of Lazarus (John 11:1–57); and, significantly, just before this, Jesus "went away again across the Jordan to the place where John at first baptized, and there he remained" (John 10:40). In a word, as Joshua crossed the Jordan before his conquests, Jesus raises Lazarus only after he has crossed the Jordan!

Consequently, the early Christians were saturated with memories of the Jordan. In what may echo a controversy

(curiously reminiscent of II Kings 5:12), Tertullian argues
that, for baptizing, the waters of the Tiber are as suitable as
the waters of the Jordan. Nevertheless, several of the ancient
liturgies speak much of the Jordan, even addressing the
water as "Jordan," or speaking of the font as the Jordan. In
the Baptistery of the Orthodox at Ravenna, the dome mo-
saic instructively depicts the baptism of Jesus. A dove hovers
over Jesus, who stands waist-deep in a stream (personified
and clearly labeled "JORDANN"), while John pours water
over Jesus' head. Interestingly, surrounding the scene, yet
flowing from it, there is a procession of the twelve apostles.[64] In Origen's *Commentary on John,* it is no surprise
that the Jordan is the river of Jesus' baptism. The Jordan is
the crucial river throughout Israel's history. Joshua, clearly
understood as a type of Jesus, led Israel through the Jordan
to the Promised Land. Elijah and Elisha crossed the Jordan;
and Naaman was restored in its waters, not in those of his
homeland. And, for Origen, even the captives who wept by
the streams of Babylon (Psalm 137) were remembering the
Jordan, the only salutary river. Therefore, he concludes, let
us now "draw from the river as much help as we require."[65]
Such, surely, is the true historical font for baptizing, giving
affluent rationale for what the Didache calls "living water";
and, within this environment, baptizing is truly the Lord's
welcome. As Yahweh saves, Jesus, like Joshua, leads the
people through the waters.

III.   If the Jordan is the background and rationale for
Christian baptizing, it also gives it shape, definition, and
direction. As an action with water, baptizing requires a place
containing water. If the earliest Christian baptisms were in

the Jordan, many of the earliest surviving baptisteries are pools, with steps leading to and from the water. They had flowing water; and they were large enough, many of them, to walk through. Often they were octagonal, symbolizing the eight saved from the ark or the "eighth day" (Lord's day, day of resurrection). They seem, as it were, to be passageways, through which those being baptized may have processed. In the truest sense, they may have been places for "rites of passage"! In any event, when many, if not all, of the baptisms were of adult converts, and when baptism marked a decisive break from Judaism or from some other religion, its sheer radicality obviously required something more momentous than birdbaths or fingerbowls. Baptizing, after all, as for Noah, Moses, and Joshua, was not a spitbath. It was not a rinsing but a rescue operation!

Thus, baptizing is something *done* to someone. While Noah built the ark, the Lord brought it safely through the waters; and Moses and Joshua *led* the people through the waters. Christian baptizing is unlike the "wash and make yourselves clean" of Isaiah, unlike the ritual cleansings of Judaism, the lustrations of Qumran, or the Jewish baptism of proselytes; for, following from the baptizing by John (which even Jesus underwent), it is always, everywhere, and for all, something done *to* someone. Consequently, the very logic of baptism continued to resist any notions of self-baptism—even when Christians became convinced that baptism was indispensable to salvation (thereby perhaps binding God to specific means?), and even when their religious nervousness led them to define martyrdom as baptism ("baptism by blood") or to speak of "emergency" baptisms. A possible exception, it seems, is the so-called "baptism by desire"; but that curious notion, if not simply an oxymoron, points toward a vacuous aridity. In this case, to comfort those who are unsure of God's free graciousness, or to appease those who believe that God is bound—and thereby limited—to specific means, or to shore up ecclesiastical power (are those three reasons interdependent?), baptism itself becomes evanescent. In any case, Christian baptizing "does not involve self-baptism, and the activity of believers recedes completely behind what is done to them."[66]

Therefore, from the time of the apostles, baptizing has always presupposed the Christian assembly. Baptizing, however conducted, was its act; and baptizing marked the entrance of the newcomers into the Christian assembly. This is clear in Acts. "Many of them believed this message and were baptized; about three thousand people were added to the group that day. . . . And every day the Lord added to their group those who were being saved" (Acts 2:41, 47, TEV). Thus, as Reginald H. Fuller observes, baptism

> brings one into an already existing community. One does not become a believer and then decide to form a society with other believers. Here, perhaps, we can see the importance of the resurrection appearances in relation to baptism. The resurrection appearances created the community. After hearing of the kerygma and faith, baptism is the means by which God inserts new members into the already existing community.[67]

Baptizing, therefore, is a *welcome through water;* it is expressed by the assembly whenever those whom the Lord is saving are welcomed into the assembly. For The Acts of the Apostles, surely, being saved, being baptized, and being added to the assembly are really one action, and all together they constitute the Lord's welcome.

I Peter, after referring to Noah, affirms that "baptism . . . now saves you also . . . [as] the pledge of a good conscience toward God . . . by the resurrection of Jesus

Christ" (I Peter 3:21, NIV). This verse has theological compactness and intensity, even though its context is obscure, its language is convoluted, several words are ambiguous, and any responsible translation requires several difficult exegetical decisions. Nevertheless, since this is, in some respects, the only actual definition of baptism within the New Testament, an interpretation needs to be given. In any event, certain dimensions deserve emphasis. First, baptism "saves" *(sōzei)*. Irrespective of how salvation is to be defined, and regardless of other ways it may be effected, baptism, at least, *saves!* Furthermore, it saves "by the resurrection" *(di' anastaseōs)*. Its authentic mystery and genuine strength is the God who "has given us new birth into a living hope through the resurrection of Jesus Christ from the dead" (I Peter 1:3, NIV). The secret of baptism's saving power is that it is anchored in God's work, not simply in ours. Therefore (and only within the sure context of God's work), baptism is a "pledge" *(eperōtēma)*. The translations are confusing. KJV has "answer," Moffatt has "prayer," Goodspeed has "craving," RSV and NEB have "appeal," JB, NAB, and NIV have "pledge," while TEV has "promise." Etymologically, there is now ample reason to think "pledge" correct. It is equivalent to the *stipulatio* in contracts; and it may be reflective of the procedure suggested in Acts 8:37 (despite the textual difficulties). It makes sense. Real welcomes do not force their way upon people; hospitality is actualized as it is accepted. In baptizing and being baptized, faith makes some difference. Therefore, because of the resurrection, baptism saves as the pledge of a good "conscience" *(syneidēseōs)*. The genitive is objective. The "conscience" is not the source of the pledge, but its promise. The promise, surely, is one of faithful integrity come what may. For I Peter, it is fidelity which persists through persecutions and suffering. The pledge of a good conscience, therefore, is the kind of commitment that promises loyalty to God's purposes. Baptism is an engagement in God's promised future. Thus, according to Bo Reicke, "If the baptismal promise is kept, the individual will really walk in the footsteps of Jesus."[68]

Nevertheless, in understanding baptism, it should be remembered that the context of this definition is a letter addressed to "a chosen race, a royal priesthood, a holy nation, God's own people, that you may declare the wonderful deeds of him who called you out of darkness into his marvelous light" (I Peter 2:9). Baptism is not a private affair. The Lord's welcome is an event for the assembly. Baptism is a public event. It is transformative, not simply for those who are being baptized, but also for those who receive newcomers into their midst. No community is ever the same after it has been invaded by the new. As those "added" bring their new experiences and gifts, the assembly itself is changed. Genuine welcomes are events, somehow affecting all who are involved; and their criterion, finally, must be whether they enhance the assembly's strengths to accomplish its tasks in the world.

Within this context of understanding, baptism is the beginning or commencement, the inauguration or initiation of the Christian life for a specific person. Being baptized is the *beginning.* It is only a beginning, but it is the beginning. Like the Jordan, it is the boundary. It marks the decisive turning, from the old and toward the new. Consequently, those who talk of being Christian, but resist baptism, may express an inarticulate but nonetheless astute sensitivity to the irretrievable commitment involved; while those who seek baptism, for themselves or others, need to be cautioned of the gravity of this step. It is only the first step, but it is

the big one. Among other things, surely, it is the recognition
of this decisiveness which has rather consistently evoked the
horror of rebaptism. After all, there is only one real beginning. Being baptized is the beginning of a *process.* Becoming a Christian is a lifelong engagement. Unlike scarifica-
tion, baptism leaves no scars. The baptismal water soon
evaporates, and it may require a lifetime for the baptism to
become fully visible! If some never begin, never get to the
Jordan, others, unfortunately, seem to stay there, and never
seem to move from it. Like pilgrims who make no progress,
they never get to Gilgal, and they miss the wonders of
Jericho, Jerusalem, and Emmaus!

Being baptized is the beginning of a process of *ministry.*
Baptism "saves," but for a purpose. Even a "royal priesthood" requires recruits! Baptism, therefore, is the incorpora-
tion of persons into a serving people; and its dimensions
have not been fully fathomed until it is understood as the
ordination of every Christian into a life of public service. As
Markus Barth puts it: "Jesus' descent into the water served
to publicize his identity and mission, to establish him in
solidarity with sinners. . . . Thus Jesus' baptism can be called
his ordination and Christian baptism is in substance the
ordination of each Christian."[69] Thus, according to Karl
Barth, "all those baptised as Christians are *eo ipso* consecrated, ordained and dedicated to the ministry of the
Church."[70] For Karl Barth, incidentally, this means that
any other, or further, ordinations lead to a "devaluation" of
baptism! He is probably right. Surely, after centuries of
clericalism, Catholic, Orthodox, and Protestant, such warn-
ings need to be pondered. Is it enough, for example, to
affirm, as Aidan Kavanagh does, that the "Church baptizes
to priesthood," while still reserving "ordination" to episco-
pacy, presbyterate, and diaconate?[71] Or does it really solve

the problems when, for American Presbyterians, *The Worshipbook* (1972) introduces "Welcome to the ministry of Jesus Christ" into the baptismal service, only to muddy the waters by inserting "Welcome to this ministry" into services for "the ordination of ministers of the word, elders, and deacons"?[72] In any event, however these issues are resolved, the direction is clear. Just as his baptism in the Jordan was the moment when Jesus' public service commenced, so being baptized is the ordination of Christians.

> Prepared for the supper of the Lamb,
> Radiant in our white robes,
> Having passed through the Red Sea,
> Let us sing to Christ the Lord.[73]

According to Gal. 3:27, "all of you who were baptized into Christ have been clothed with Christ" (NIV). This verse itself may come from an early baptismal liturgy;[74] but we cannot be sure what it actually indicates historically. Which came first, action or idea? If nudity was customary in baptism, those being baptized may have put on a new garment when they came from the waters, and Paul simply theologizes from custom; or, if the metaphor of being "clothed with Christ" came first, it may itself have become clothed with custom. In either case, whichever came first, before long Christians were wearing white garments as they came from baptism and were given places in the assembly. The *Te Deum laudamus* declares: "The white-robed army of martyrs praise you." The word, of course, is *candidatus;* and among the possible meanings of the white robe, it may be remembered, is a custom by which, in the Roman Empire, a person announced "candidacy" for public office by appearing in a white toga. The clothing after baptism may derive from some such custom; but whether this is the historically correct explanation or not, it is profoundly consistent with a significant dimension of baptismal theology. Unlike the initiatory rites of the mystery religions, Christian baptizing was an event with immense social consequences.[75] Thus, according to Hans Dieter Betz, the baptismal liturgy

> would communicate information to the newly initiated, telling them of their eschatological status before God . . . and also informing them how this status affects, and in fact changes their social, cultural, and religious self-understanding, as well as their responsibilities in the here-and-now.[76]

Along such lines, parenthetically, it is noteworthy that John Calvin considered that public office "is a calling [*vocatio*], not only holy and lawful before God, but also the most sacred and by far the most honorable of all callings in the whole life of mortal men."[77]

The baptized "have been clothed with Christ," and this affects both them and the assembly. The assembly is never the same again, for the new have been added; and the assembly is not free to pick and choose among those who have been given the Lord's welcome and are clothed with Christ. Consequently, many customary patterns of ecclesiastical discipline are truly suspect. The assembly, not the baptized, has the burden of proof. For example, lest the host be offended at the way welcomed guests are treated, none of those so welcomed is to be kept from the feast. After all, butlers and waiters are not the true masters of the guest lists. Consequently, even to make a question of intercommunion smacks of a faithless repudiation of somebody's baptism; and it makes a hostage of the host! Ultimately, it is to strip and rob Christians of the garment given them by Christ, abandoning them to the whims of priests and Levites.

Furthermore, in an assembly to which Jews and Greeks,

slave and free, male and female, have been welcomed, all of
the old lines, which society so delights in drawing, have been
erased. Baptism is the only boundary left! And among the
baptized, no distinctions, whether from racism, classism, or
sexism, are permitted. This means, among other things,
that, although any "ordination" beyond baptism may be
questionable, to allow ordination to men, while denying it
to women, is to threaten the very meaning of baptism. After
all, if the baptized are truly clothed with Christ, how can
anyone tell whether they are men or women? Christianity
was born from a religion (Judaism) which had many fundamental rites and rights for men, but few for women; but
Christianity took the revolutionary step of incorporating
both men and women in baptism. Hence, so long as baptism
is the norm, the assembly is obliged to live and pattern its
life faithfully from, by, and with the consequences of receiving baptism, and all the baptized, seriously.

IV. To baptize, or to be baptized, *celebrates* the
Lord's welcome. From one perspective, baptism is the final
topic in understanding worship, for baptism is that gracious
activity in which those who are being saved to serve are
"added" to an assembly that gathers, celebrates time, shares
feasts, and serves. Their hospitality, their willingness to
honor and express the Lord's welcome, is a measure of their
grace and gratitude; and it indicates their future. Finally, the
assembly must baptize or die! From another perspective,
baptism is the beginning. Those who are welcomed know
themselves as commencing a life with Jesus and among his
assembled people. For such persons, baptism is the beginning of a new future. It is their first step on the path of

pilgrims. In a way, therefore, baptism is the activity of grace *par excellence.*

To baptize, or to be baptized, *acknowledges* that we live our lives in a God-given history. To be human is to have a history. Our lives are defined by where we have come from and where we are going. Baptism gives us a new past. As H. Richard Niebuhr so clearly puts it:

> When men enter into a new community they not only share the present life of their new companions but also adopt as their own the past history of their fellows. So immigrants do not become true members of the American community until they have learned to call the Pilgrims and the men of 1776 their fathers and to regard the torment of the Civil War as somehow their own.[78]

In this sense, for many Americans, the Atlantic was the boundary, and the crossing of the waters was a definitive event.

> O God, beneath thy guiding hand
> Our exiled fathers crossed the sea;
> And when they trod the wintry strand,
> With prayer and psalm they worshipped thee.[79]

Like poetry for Rainer Maria Rilke, baptism is "the past that breaks out in our hearts." In baptism, the baptizers and the baptized are reminded of their past and its promise; in baptism, they acknowledge, together, the beginning of a new future.

To baptize, or to be baptized, *rehearses* life as it is meant to be, full of promise, enriched with vital memories, and open to the future. It is a shared life, open to surprise, the never-ending surprises of grace. As the Lord's welcome, expressed in the assembly, baptism rehearses a willingness to

receive, as well as to give. In baptizing, the assembly lives
its need for the new, the challenging, the energizing, the
sometimes quite threatening, new, the emerging way; and,
in being baptized, each unique person lives her or his need
for the nurture, support, and demands of others. In baptism,
communities and persons make promises to one another,
thereby rehearsing the very center and hope of covenantal
living. After all, the original "home" of baptizing is not the
mystery cults, with their private and esoteric rites and purposes; rather, its formative paradigms are the entrance of a
people into the Promised Land and a leader who is crucified
because he is a public threat to the established cultural,
political, and religious orders. In baptism a faithful assembly
discovers ways to the covenantal renewal of human society.

To baptize, or be baptized, *proclaims* that all our lives are
planted in grace and constituted by promises. Baptism tells
the truth about reality; it is the sign of covenant in our
midst. It is the public announcement of the Lord's welcome,
the adventurous, winsome, and exhilarating summons into
the covenanted life of the Promised Land. Therefore, since
actions speak more loudly than words:

> Baptism into Christ demands enough water to die in, oil so
> fragrant and in such quantity that it becomes the Easter
> aroma, kisses and *abrazos,* bread and wine enough to feed
> and rejoice hearts. And rooms of glory filled with life rather
> than crumpled vestments and stacks of folding chairs.[80]

Gloriously, in circumstances such as these, "every day the
Lord added to their group those who were being saved."

NOTES

Scripture quotations, unless otherwise noted, are from the Revised Standard Version. Other versions used are Jerusalem Bible (JB), New American Bible (NAB), New English Bible (NEB), New International Version (NIV), and Today's English Version (TEV).

1. *The Ancient Near East: An Anthology of Texts and Pictures,* ed. by James B. Pritchard (Princeton University Press, 1958), p. 36.

2. *Ioannis Calvini opera quae supersunt omnia* (in *Corpus Reformatorum,* ed. by G. Baum et al.), 59 vols. (Braunschweig: Schwetschke, 1863–1900), 11:486.

3. Evelyn Underhill, *Worship* (London: James Nisbet & Co., 1936), pp. 5, 61.

4. Langdon Gilkey, *Catholicism Confronts Modernity: A Protestant View* (Seabury Press, 1975), p. 180.

5. Ferdinand Hahn, *The Worship of the Early Church,* tr. by David E. Green (Fortress Press, 1973), pp. 38–39.

6. Suzanne K. Langer, *Philosophy in a New Key: A Study in the Symbolism of Reason, Rite, and Art,* 3d ed. (Harvard University Press, 1957), p. 45.

7. *Man: The Journal of the Royal Anthropological Institute,* N.S., Vol. 1 (March 1966), pp. 60–74.

8. Edmund Leach, *Culture and Communication: The Logic by Which Symbols Are Connected* (London: Cambridge University Press, 1976), p. 45.

9. *The Westminster Directory, Being A Directory for the Publique Worship of God in the Three Kingdomes,* ed. by Ian Bre

ward. Grove Liturgical Study No. 21 (Bramcote, Nottingham-shire: Grove Books, 1980), p. 23.

10. Clifford Geertz, *The Interpretation of Cultures: Selected Essays* (Basic Books, 1973), p. 90.

11. Ibid., p. 122.

12. Raimundo Panikkar, *Worship and Secular Man* (Orbis Books, 1973), p. 89.

13. Gerhard Delling, *Worship in the New Testament*, tr. by Percy Scott (London: Darton, Longman & Todd, 1962), p. 10.

14. T. S. Eliot, "The Dry Salvages" (from *Four Quartets*), *The Complete Poems and Plays, 1909–1950* (Harcourt, Brace and Co. 1952), p. 136.

15. Robert J. Ledogar, *Acknowledgement: Praise-Verbs in the Early Greek Anaphora* (Rome: Casa Editrice Herder, 1968), p. 167.

16. Karl Rahner, *Theological Investigations*, Vol. 14, *Ecclesiology, Questions in the Church, the Church in the World*, tr. by David Bourke (London: Darton, Longman & Todd, 1976), pp. 166–170.

17. Josef Pieper, *In Tune with the World: A Theory of Festivity*, tr. by Richard and Clara Winston (Harcourt, Brace and World, 1965), p. 23.

18. *The Mishnah*, tr. by Herbert Danby (London: Oxford University Press, 1933), p. 450.

19. *The Babylonian Talmud, Seder Zera'im, Berakoth*, ed. by I. Epstein (London: Soncino Press, 1948), p. 23.

20. *Didascalia Apostolorum*, tr. and ed. by R. Hugh Connolly (Oxford: Oxford University Press, 1929), p. 124.

21. William James, *The Varieties of Religious Experience* (Longmans, Green & Co., 1902), p. 31.

22. John Locke, *A Letter Concerning Toleration*, ed. by Patrick Romanell (Liberal Arts Press, 1950), p. 20.

23. Didache 9:4 (author's translation). For a critical text, see *Die apostolischen Väter*, ed. by F. X. Funk, K. Bihlmeyer, and W.

Schneemelcher, 3d ed. (Tübingen: J. C. B. Mohr [Paul Siebeck], 1970), p. 6.

24. Peter Brown, *The World of Late Antiquity: From Marcus Aurelius to Muhammad* (London: Thames and Hudson, 1971), p. 66.

25. Plato, *Laws* II.653. *The Collected Dialogues of Plato, Including the Letters*, ed. by Edith Hamilton and Huntington Cairns, Bollingen Series LXXI (Princeton University Press, 1961), p. 1250.

26. Quoted in *Encyclopaedia Judaica*, 1971 ed., art. "Sabbath," by Louis Jacobs.

27. Abraham Joshua Heschel, *The Sabbath* (Farrar, Straus & Young, 1951), p. 14.

28. Ignatius of Antioch, To the Magnesians 9:1 (Lightfoot); *Die apostolischen Väter*, ed. by F. X. Funk, K. Bihlmeyer, and W. Schneemelcher, 3d ed. (Tübingen: J. C. B. Mohr [Paul Siebeck], 1970), p. 91.

29. Justin Martyr, *First Apology* 67. *The Faith of the Early Fathers*, Vol. I, ed. by William A. Jurgens (Liturgical Press, 1970), p. 56. Justin's Greek text appears in *PREX EUCHARISTICA: textus e variis liturgiis antiquioribus selecti*, ed. by Anton Hänggi and Irmgard Pahl (Fribourg: Éditions Universitaires Fribourg Suisse, 1968), pp. 68–72.

30. Basil the Great, *On the Holy Spirit* 27.66. Basil's Greek text appears in Willy Rordorf, *Sabbat und Sonntag in der Alten Kirche* (Zürich: Theologischer Verlag, 1972), pp. 188–191.

31. Martin Buber, *Tales of the Hasidim: The Early Masters*, tr. by Olga Marx (Farrar, Straus & Young, 1947), pp. v–vi.

32. *Encyclopaedia Britannica*, 1962 ed., art. "Drama," by Ivor Brown.

33. Mary Douglas, Introduction to Jessica Kuper (ed.), *The Anthropologists' Cookbook* (Universe Books, 1977), p. 7.

34. Émile Durkheim, *The Elementary Forms of the Religious Life*, tr. by Joseph Ward Swain (London: George Allen & Unwin, 1915), p. 378.

35. Mary Douglas, *Implicit Meanings: Essays in Anthropology* (London: Routledge & Kegan Paul, 1975), p. 256.

36. Octavio Paz, *Alternating Current,* tr. by Helen R. Lane (Viking Press, 1973), p. 100.

37. Gustaf Dalman, *Jesus-Jeshua: Studies in the Gospels,* tr. by Paul P. Levertoff (1922; E.T., Macmillan Co., 1929), pp. 134–135.

38. Joseph Heinemann, *Prayer in the Talmud: Forms and Patterns,* Studia Judaica, Vol. 9 (Berlin and New York: Walter de Gruyter & Co., 1977), p. 18.

39. Lionel Blue and June Rose, *A Taste of Heaven: Adventures in Food and Faith* (Templegate Publishers, 1978), p. 33.

40. Dalman, *Jesus-Jeshua,* p. 178.

41. Ernst Käsemann, *New Testament Questions of Today,* tr. by W. J. Montague (Fortress Press, 1969), pp. 188–195.

42. George E. Mendenhall, "Biblical Faith and Cultic Evolution," *The Lutheran Quarterly,* Vol. 5 (1953), p. 240.

43. Jeannette Mirsky, *Houses of God* (University of Chicago Press, 1965), p. 118.

44. Berthe M. Marti, "Proskynesis and Adorare," *Language: Journal of the Linguistic Society of America,* Vol. 12 (1936), pp. 272–282.

45. Bo Reicke, "Some Reflections on Worship in the New Testament," in A. J. B. Higgins (ed.), *New Testament Essays: Studies in Memory of Thomas Walter Manson* (Manchester: Manchester University Press, 1959), p. 196.

46. I Thess. 5:26 has "Greet all the brethren with a holy kiss" (RSV); and I Peter 5:14 has "Greet one another with the kiss of love" (RSV). See Delling, *Worship in the New Testament,* p. 170.

47. *Tertullian's Tract on The Prayer,* tr. and ed. by Ernest Evans (London: S.P.C.K., 1953), p. 22.

48. Hugh M. Scott, "The Place of *oikodomē* in New Testament Worship," *The Princeton Theological Review,* Vol. 2 (1904), p. 403.

49. *The Enchiridion of Erasmus,* tr. and ed. by Raymond Hime-lick (Indiana University Press, 1963), p. 122.

50. Ernst Haenchen, *The Acts of the Apostles: A Commentary,* tr. by Bernard Noble et al. (Westminster Press, 1971), p. 191.

51. William Nagel, *Geschichte des christlichen Gottesdienstes,* 2d ed. (Berlin: Walter de Gruyter & Co., 1970), p. 20.

52. Hans Conzelmann, *1 Corinthians: A Commentary on the First Epistle to the Corinthians,* tr. by James W. Leitch, ed. by George W. MacRae; Hermeneia (Fortress Press, 1975), p. 204; Günther Bornkamm, *Early Christian Experience,* tr. by Paul L. Hammer (Harper & Row, 1970), pp. 161–179; Ferdinand Hahn, *The Worship of the Early Church,* tr. by David E. Green (Fortress Press, 1973), pp. 68–73; and Eduard Schweizer, "The Service of Worship: An Exposition of I Corinthians 14," *Interpretation,* Vol. 13 (1959), pp. 400–408.

53. Quoted in Adrienne Rich, *On Lies, Secrets, and Silence: Selected Prose 1966–1978* (W. W. Norton & Co., 1979), p. 185.

54. "So important was this response by the congregation consid-ered, that in the large Synagogue in Alexandria, where there was a difficulty for all the members of the congregation to hear when the end of a prayer or a benediction was reached, an official stood up on the platform in the centre of the Synagogue and waved a flag as a sign to the congregation to make the response" (W. O. E. Oesterley, *The Jewish Background of the Christian Liturgy*, p. 71; London: Oxford University Press, 1925; repr. by Peter Smith).

55. A few paragraphs in this chapter are adapted from the author's article, "Have All the Seas Gone Dry?" *Reformed Liturgy and Music,* Vol. 15 (1981).

56. Thomas Y. Canby, "Our Most Precious Resource: Water," *The National Geographic Magazine,* Vol. 158 (August 1980), p. 148.

57. Philip Larkin, *The Whitsun Weddings* (London: Faber & Faber, 1964), p. 20.

58. Aidan Kavanagh, *The Shape of Baptism: The Rite of Chris-*

tian Initiation (Pueblo Publishing Co., 1978), p. 29.

59. Nelson Glueck, *The River Jordan* (McGraw-Hill Book Co., 1968), p. xv.

60. Professor Edward F. Campbell, Jr., graciously suggested this reference, although he did not know to what use it might be put.

61. Glueck, *The River Jordan*, pp. 206–207.

62. Karl Barth, *Church Dogmatics* IV/4, *The Christian Life* (Fragment): *Baptism as the Foundation of the Christian Life*, tr. by G. W. Bromiley (Edinburgh: T. & T. Clark, 1969), p. 45.

63. Raymond E. Brown, *The Gospel According to John*, Vol. I, The Anchor Bible (Doubleday & Co., 1966), p. 44.

64. *Age of Spirituality: Late Antique and Early Christian Art, Third to Seventh Century*, ed. by Kurt Weitzmann (Metropolitan Museum of Art, 1979), p. 659.

65. Origen, *Commentary on John; The Ante-Nicene Fathers*, Vol. 9, ed. by Allan Menzies (Christian Literature Co., 1896), pp. 370–375. For a critical text, see *Origène, Commentaire sur S. Jean*, ed. by Cécile Blanc. Sources Chrétiennes, Vol. 157 (Paris: Éditions du Cerf, 1970), pp. 285–319.

66. Ernst Käsemann, *Commentary on Romans*, tr. and ed. by Geoffrey W. Bromiley (Wm. B. Eerdmans Publishing Co., 1980), p. 164.

It is unfortunate that Karl Barth's provocative and influential discussions of baptism (*Church Dogmatics* IV/4) are not informed by a genuine interest in liturgical actions. Barth, like Zwingli before him, is relatively inattentive to rites. Here, as elsewhere, he seems to have an eye only for words, and not for actions as well. Hence, for him, it is only mildly significant that baptism is not self-administered. Perhaps in his refusal to think grace as mediated (whether through human events, persons, or things), he thinks grace invisible!

Clearly, the heart of Barth's argument is founded upon a distinction, stressed earlier by Gerhard Kittel, between "baptism with water" and "baptism with the Holy Spirit." Thus, perhaps from a mountainous fear of synergism, Barth draws a strict line (verging on something akin to Nestorianism) between God's action and human action. Consequently, for Barth, the action of the community, while "indispensable" to "baptism with water," really "takes second place to the action of the candidate and simply assists this" (Barth, ibid., p. 50). Thus, if Käsemann's reading of Paul is correct, the contrast between Paul and Barth is startling, especially since it hinges on the understanding of Romans! Here, surely, where his whole theological perspective is at stake, Barth may be farther from the New Testament than are those who, while normally baptizing converts, also allow for the baptizing of infants. The exegetical issue is whether Spirit and water may be separated so neatly; and, therefore, whether the Spirit is to be understood as using the assembly and its baptizing with water to bestow grace. On this point, it is surely worthwhile to consider the criticism of Kittel by an English Baptist exegete, G. R. Beasley-Murray. Speaking of Kittel, he writes: "In his view the New Testament never affirms that water baptism bestows the baptism of the Spirit or calls forth any spiritual change; it is solely a witness to an inner change that has already taken place. This, of course, is the position that has been adopted by many Free Churchmen, but as an exegetical judgment it is hardly to be received. On the contrary, in the Acts and Epistles baptism is the supreme moment of the impartation of the Spirit and of the work of the Spirit in the believer" (G. R. Beasley-Murray, *Baptism in the New Testament,* p. 275; St. Martin's Press, 1962).

Nevertheless, despite the neatness of his arguments, even Barth must have had an inkling of some shadowy edges to his own logic. Otherwise, his own refusal even to consider "rebaptism" (Barth, ibid., p. 189) wanders like a vagrant, floating free from any moorings in his theology of baptism. Consequently, although both Barth and Beasley-Murray struggle to be both exegetically sound and theologically coherent, their incoherences may prove finally as instructive as their coherences. Beasley-Murray admits that baptism with water really effects something, but argues that those baptized in infancy should be rebaptized when they become believers; Barth argues that baptism with water really effects nothing, but admits that those who were baptized before they became believers should not be rebaptized. They appear to be at one, however, in their belief that everything really hinges upon the faith of the individual person, baptized or not. Neither of them, therefore, seems really open to what may be the theological import, extending even to baptism, of Mark 2:5 (and parallels): "And when Jesus saw *their* faith, he said to the paralytic, 'My son, your sins are forgiven.' " Emphasis added!

67. Reginald H. Fuller, "Christian Initiation in the New Testament," in *Made, Not Born: New Perspectives on Christian Initiation and the Catechumenate,* from the Murphy Center for Liturgical Research (University of Notre Dame Press, 1976), p. 13.

68. Bo Reicke, *The Epistles of James, Peter, and Jude.* The Anchor Bible (Doubleday & Co., 1964), p. 115.

69. *The Interpreter's Dictionary of the Bible,* Supplementary Volume (Abingdon Press, 1976), art. "Baptism," by Markus Barth.

70. Karl Barth, *Church Dogmatics* IV/4, p. 201.

71. Kavanagh, *The Shape of Baptism,* p. 188.

72. *The Worshipbook* (Westminster Press, 1972), pp. 46 and 94. The problems, it may be noted, are not only those of baptism versus ordination; for when an infant has been baptized, the phrase "Welcome to the ministry of Jesus Christ" is omitted, although the preposition "of" could here be read as a felicitous ambiguity! When all the dust has settled, and if baptism is to be understood properly as ordination, it may be that the determinative question concerning the baptism of infants is whether it is appropriate to ordain them for what may only be understood as involuntary servitude. Pastorally, therefore, in a world where baptism is widely misunderstood, either as a social formality or as insurance against damnation, and where baptism may have lost its meaning for many, in part because there are too many baptisms, not too few, and where being baptized takes place often quite easily and inconspicuously; pastors may need to inquire, even

strenuously, whether those who wish their children baptized really understand the task, as well as the gift, that they would thrust upon their children.

73. These lines, translated from the ancient Latin hymn *"Ad cenam agni providi,"* appear in O. B. Hardison, Jr., *Christian Rite and Christian Drama in the Middle Ages: Essays in the Origin and Early History of Modern Drama* (Johns Hopkins Press, 1965), p. 95. A critical edition of the Latin text is given in A. S. Walpole, *Early Latin Hymns* (Cambridge University Press, 1922; repr., Hildesheim: Georg Ohms Verlagsbuchhandlung, 1966), pp. 350–353.

74. Hans Dieter Betz, *Galatians: A Commentary on Paul's Letter to the Churches in Galatia;* Hermeneia (Fortress Press, 1979), p. 32.

75. George Every, *The Baptismal Sacrifice* (London: SCM Press, 1959), p. 25.

76. Betz, *Galatians,* p. 184.

77. *Institution of the Christian Religion* (1536 edition), tr. by Ford Lewis Battles (John Knox Press, 1975), p. 288. The Latin text of this sentence (which was continued into the 1559 edition of the *Institutes*) appears in *Joannis Calvini Opera Selecta,* Vol. I, ed. by Peter Barth (Munich: Chr. Kaiser, 1926), p. 216.

78. H. Richard Niebuhr, *The Meaning of Revelation* (Macmillan Co., 1941), p. 115.

79. Leonard Bacon, who was pastor of Center Church, New Haven, wrote this hymn in 1838 to celebrate the 200th anniversary of the founding of New Haven, Connecticut. See *Hymnal for Colleges and Schools,* ed. by E. Harold Geer (Yale University Press, 1956), p. 332, and the appended note by Luther Noss.

80. Kavanagh, *The Shape of Baptism,* pp. 179–180.

FOR FURTHER READING

GENERAL

Davies, J. G., ed. *The Westminster Dictionary of Liturgy and Worship* (first published as *A Dictionary of Liturgy and Worship,* 1972). Westminster Press, 1979.

Jones, Cheslyn; Wainwright, Geoffrey; and Yarnold, Edward, eds. *The Study of Liturgy.* New York: Oxford University Press, 1978.

Parrinder, Geoffrey. *Worship in the World's Religions.* 2d ed. London: Sheldon Press, 1974.

White, James F. *Introduction to Christian Worship.* Abingdon Press, 1980.

Chapter I. WHY WORSHIP?

Geertz, Clifford. *The Interpretation of Cultures: Selected Essays.* Basic Books, 1973.

Panikkar, Raimundo. *Worship and Secular Man: An Essay on the Liturgical Nature of Man, Considering Secularization as a Major Phenomenon of Our Time and Worship as an Apparent Fact of All Times: A Study Towards an Integral Anthropology.* Orbis Books, 1973.

Pieper, Josef. *In Tune with the World: A Theory of Festivity.* Tr. by Richard and Clara Winston. Harcourt, Brace and World, 1965.

Smart, Ninian. *The Concept of Worship.* London: Macmillan Press, 1972.

Chapter II. THE LORD'S ASSEMBLY

Audet, Jean-Paul. *Structures of Christian Priesthood: A Study of Home, Marriage, and Celibacy in the Pastoral Service of the Church.* Tr. by Rosemary Sheed. Macmillan Co., 1968.

Gustafson, James. *Treasure in Earthen Vessels: The Church as a Human Community.* Harper & Brothers, 1961.

Küng, Hans. *The Church.* Tr. by Ray and Rosaleen Ockenden. Sheed & Ward, 1967.

Luckmann, Thomas. *The Invisible Religion: The Problem of Religion in Modern Society.* Macmillan Co., 1967.

Chapter III. THE LORD'S DAY

Heschel, Abraham Joshua. *The Sabbath: Its Meaning for Modern Man.* Farrar, Straus & Young, 1951.

Power, David, ed. *The Times of Celebration.* Concilium, Vol. 142. Seabury Press, 1981.

Rordorf, Willy. *Sunday: The History of the Day of Rest and Worship in the Earliest Centuries of the Christian Church.* Tr. by A. A. K. Graham. Westminster Press, 1968.

Warner, W. Lloyd. *The Family of God: A Symbolic Study of Christian Life in America.* Yale University Press, 1961.

Chapter IV. THE LORD'S FEAST

Jasper, R. C. D., and Cuming, G. J., eds. *Prayers of the Eucharist: Early and Reformed.* 2d ed. Oxford University Press, 1980.

Kuper, Jessica, ed. *The Anthropologists' Cookbook.* Introduction by Mary Douglas. Universe Books, 1977.

Marxsen, Willi. *The Beginnings of Christology; Together with The Lord's Supper as a Christological Problem.* Tr. by Paul J. Achtemeier and Lorenz Nieting. Introduction by John Reumann. Fortress Press, 1979.

Schweizer, Eduard. *The Lord's Supper According to the New Testament.* Tr. by James M. Davis. Fortress Press, 1967.

Chapter V. THE LORD'S SERVICE

Conzelmann, Hans. *1 Corinthians: A Commentary on the First Epistle to the Corinthians.* Hermeneia. Tr. by James W. Leitch. Ed. by George W. MacRae. Fortress Press, 1975.

Hahn, Ferdinand. *The Worship of the Early Church.* Tr. by David E. Green. Ed. with an introduction by John Reumann. Fortress Press, 1973.

Oesterley, W. O. E. *The Jewish Background of the Christian Liturgy.* Oxford University Press, 1925; repr. by Peter Smith.

Schweizer, Eduard. *Church Order in the New Testament.* Studies in Biblical Theology, No. 32. Tr. by Frank Clarke. London: SCM Press, 1961.

Chapter VI. THE LORD'S WELCOME

Barth, Karl. *Church Dogmatics.* Vol. IV, *The Doctrine of Reconciliation;* Part 4, *The Christian Life* (Fragment): *Baptism as the Foundation of the Christian Life.* Tr. by G. W. Bromiley. Edinburgh: T. & T. Clark, 1969.

Beasley-Murray, G. R. *Baptism in the New Testament.* St. Martin's Press, 1962.

The Murphy Center for Liturgical Research. *Made, Not Born: New Perspectives on Christian Initiation and the Catechumenate.* University of Notre Dame Press, 1976.

Whitaker, E. C. *Documents of the Baptismal Liturgy.* 2d ed. London: S.P.C.K., 1970.

INDEX OF BIBLICAL REFERENCES

INDEX OF PERSONS

INDEX OF SUBJECTS